BABY BOOTCAMP

Sleep Training for a Happy Healthy Baby

RUTH THUNDER

TABLE OF CONTENTS

INTRODUCTION

It's 2 am.

I am in the hallway crying; my baby is in his room screaming. I feel like I'm failing miserably at this whole mom thing. How long am I just supposed to let him 'cry it out?' I keep asking myself over and over.

It feels like hours of just sitting here. The crying feels like it's been going on for days. In reality, the clock shows just 3 minutes passed, but I can't take it anymore.

I rushed into my son's room. Scoop him up and rock him peacefully to sleep. I gently lay him back down and quietly back out of his room. Just as I take two steps towards my own room, the crying starts again. When does this get easier?

This is a typical situation for many first-time parents. This was me. Despite all my experience as a pediatric sleep specialist, I was up multiple nights with my little one, well after he was 9 months old. There's a big difference knowing the research about sleep behavior, and being right there in the middle of it - experiencing the stress, anxiety, and chaos.

When I had my first son, David, we were sure we would be an instant success story with sleep training. I had completely different views back then than I do today. I was definitely relying too much on research and methodology, without giving much consideration to the fact that my son was his own unique little person.

The middle-of-the-night wakings. The self-doubt. The wishful thinking that this little bundle of joy, who used to sleep all the time when we first brought him home, would just be a good sleeper. Though I knew that babies didn't sleep through the night on their own for at least a few months, it didn't stop me from believing that we would be the exception. We weren't. I was struggling through the days with the bare minimum of sleep. "All new parents struggle with sleep," I was reassured.

This isn't how sleep should be; for you as a parent or for your baby. Sleep should not be an experience that your baby or you dread because of these tears and resistance. It should be a time, instead, where you are bonding and creating positive memories while also providing your baby with essential life lessons. Healthy sleep patterns are taught, and not automatically perfected by babies.

Almost all parents struggle with some form of sleep issues with their children, whether it is their first or seventh. I wasn't alone in my struggles, I now understand. Every baby is different and what works blissfully for one family might be a complete disaster for another. I learned this the hard way.

When I finally decided that the method we were using with David wasn't working, I had to go back to the drawing board. There had to be something I was missing. That something was what changed the way I looked at baby sleep patterns. While I was busy doing everything my research and years of experience told me to do, I neglected to include what actually does come naturally - nurturing, love, and bonding time.

When I began to incorporate both modern-day, gentle approaches, with old-school methods to sleep training, what resulted was miraculous. Though we didn't have overnight success, we did have far less stressful bedtimes. We had more peaceful late-night wakings and after a short amount of time, we had a happy little sleeper. I used this approach with my other two children. The routine for each was changed to accommodate their own personal needs. When we did, we had fewer tears when it came to sleeping through the night.

When I look back and think of the nightmare we endured for almost the first full year of our first son's life, it pains me to know that this is what many first-time parents think is the norm. For them, bedtime is considered a chore and burden. It is stressful for parent and baby, and it shouldn't be. There is another way. A unique method is available that involves happy memories and precious moments - not tears, screams, and sleep deprivation.

This is what has driven me to write this book. Once we began adopting this new approach of sleep coaching with my son, I began to teach it to families I worked with. There were no strict guidelines to follow and, ultimately, there was minimal resistance to bedtime. Success story after success story proved to me that what we thought we knew about baby sleep is far from what our babies actually need.

I wrote this book so parents can find the answers they have been looking for - one that doesn't involve hours of screaming and crying, stress, or discouragement. I'll be sharing my own personal experiences and those of clients I have worked with who have also struggled with different baby sleep issues. I'll also highlight how the tips and techniques provided in this book have helped a variety of families come up with a sleep training method that fits their needs. More importantly, in this book we'll go through different ideas that you can try – and, if done consistently, I think you'll find they'll make a huge difference in the quality of your baby's sleep and in the quality of your life as a loving parent.

What to Expect

This book will give you information about what you can expect from the first day you bring your baby home all the way up until they are of school age. You will know when to expect sleep issues to arise and how you can handle them with compassion and confidence. You will learn what you can begin to do from day one to teach your baby healthy sleep habits that they will carry with them for the rest of their lives.

There are chapters dedicated to understanding what internal and external factors can hinder your baby's natural sleep cycle. These chapters also provide you with advice for setting up the safest and most comfortable sleep environment for your baby, and what you can do to encourage your child to sleep independently. You will find examples of routines, sleep schedules, and suggestions for calming your baby when they are overtired or stimulated.

The new approaches to sleep that you will discover in this book do not just focus on getting your baby to sleep. You will also learn how a gentle approach to teaching your child healthy sleep habits allows everyone to enjoy and cherish bedtime routines. For 20 years now, I have had the pleasure of working with families from all different backgrounds and cultures, successfully addressing and resolving their sleep/bedtime issues. The methods you will find in this book will help you regulate your baby's sleeping schedule without having to hear your baby cry-it-out and without excessive stress on mom or dad.

In this book, I'll lay out the foundation for how you can develop a plan that takes into account more than just getting the baby to sleep through the night. You will learn how to really connect with your baby so that you can work with them, instead of forcing them to follow a schedule that will only bring about resistance.

The new approaches you will discover about baby sleep will give you a fresh perspective of what normal sleep is. You will be able to create your own new normal, where you and your baby get the quality sleep you both need.

If you are ready to dive into the root cause of your baby's sleep and commit to a nurturing and effective plan, you only need to turn the page to be on your way to more restful nights.

CHAPTER 1:

BABY SLEEP: THEORY AND PRACTICE

It feels as though I haven't slept in months. When we first brought Hayden home, she was sleeping all the time. The multiple night wakings didn't have as much of an effect. I knew during the day I'd be able to catch up on the sleep I was missing from feeding her all night. She is now 9 months old and the day-time sleep has diminished, but the middle of the night wakings have not. I'm exhausted all the time. How am I supposed to get the sleep I need if she isn't sleeping through the night? My sister-in-law just had a baby and gloats about how her son has been sleeping through the night since day one. What am I doing wrong? - Abigale, new mom.

Abigale's story is similar to other parents I have worked with. Either they hear about a friend's or relative's baby who has been sleeping through the night from day one or they are questioning what they are doing wrong. A newborn baby who sleeps through the night is not the norm. If another parent is telling you this, rest assured it is most likely not their reality. So, before you begin to beat yourself up and exhaust yourself, let's gain a better understanding of your baby's sleep. Without this understanding, you are bound to run into more complications as your child grows.

The first thing that needs to be addressed is how your baby's sleep differs from your own. New parents are often told, for instance, how many hours their child is supposed to sleep. This is rarely explained as to what it means exactly. Our natural biological clocks let us know when we should be sleeping and when we should awake but this is not yet established in a baby. This small bit of information, that many parents are never made aware of, can help you avoid setting expectations that your baby is just not developmentally ready to adhere to.

In this chapter, we will go over what these sleep cycles are like for adults, young children, and your newborn. You will also learn what the sleep process entails and what you can do from the first day to begin to build healthy sleep habits, even before your baby's internal clock comes into play.

What to be Aware of at the Beginning

Adults cycle through sleep stages in which the activity in our brain changes and the body heals and restores itself. Like essential vitamins and minerals, sleep is essential to our health. As we grow from our teenage years to our older adult lives, sleep is one of the first things we tend to sacrifice to get more done during the day. Whether this means staying up late to study, or staying up all night to party, sleep loses its significance when our day becomes filled with 'stuff.'

Understanding the nature of sleep and what the body undertakes while you are asleep can lead to a better appreciation of how our body needs this resting period. This is a time where we can conserve our energy and let our body and brain to restore itself. During this time, also, growth hormones are released and slow sleep waves allow the brain to organize and make new memory categories.

Despite what many believe, sleep is not a time where the body and brain ‘shuts off.' During sleep, the brain goes through a number of different activity levels; in some stages the activity is quite intense. Knowing how the brain is functioning during these stages of sleep can help identify sleep issues that can cause you to wake up suddenly. These can also be a guiding post to how your little one will sleep.

When your baby is only a few weeks old, broken sleep is going to occur, and this is okay. Though your newborn will sleep for a majority of the day, they are doing this in shorter windows of time. It is when children are older that this broken sleep can become an issue, especially for those children of school-age whose sleep, or lack of, can have a negative impact on their ability to learn and function in school appropriately.

For young children, sleep is a time for promoting physical growth and for organizing new skills and memories that will be useful later in life. This is true for your newborn as well.

Historical Knowledge

Up until the 1930s, sleep was thought to be an inactive state. With the development of electroencephalograms (EEGs), scientists were able to discover that sleep was not inactive, but that the brain was actually fully active during sleep. It was through these first studies done using EEGs that two distinct sleep stages were discovered.

Rapid eye movement (REM) and non-rapid-eye-movement (NREM) showed patterns in sleep where brain waves would change frequency and rhythm.

In REM sleep there are small, yet fast brain waves going off in the brain. It is in REM sleep that we dream, which accounts for why our arms and legs go dormant when we are in this sleep stage.

NREM consists of three different sub-stages. From stage one to three the brain slows down. In stage three NREM sleep, we are in a deep slow-wave sleep. Adults cycle through the three NREM stages and one REM stage. This is not always done in consecutive order; generally, we have to go through the first three NREM stages and then bounce back to stage two NREM before we ever reach REM sleep. Adults repeat these cycles two or three times throughout the night; each time they enter into REM sleep the cycle tends to lengthen.

There are a number of factors that can impact the quality of an adult's sleep cycle. These factors can be due to sudden life experience (like stress from losing a job) or can be things that have become a habit since early childhood. When we grow up with poor sleeping behaviors as children, this impacts our quality of sleep as we become older. Developing healthy sleep habits and behaviors when we are younger, even as babies, can ensure that, when we grow older, we get the quality and quantity of sleep that we need.

There are plenty of misconceptions that new parents have when it comes to newborn and baby sleep. Addressing these will help you maintain a realistic view on how to handle your baby's sleep issues.

There is a great deal of debate that arises when talking about sleep problems in infants and children. For decades, sleep had been approached with the same understanding of teaching appropriate behaviors to children. This approach typically revolves around ignoring the undesired behaviors. The child will then find it less desirable to behave that way because they are not getting the attention they are seeking from that behavior. However, sleep is not a 'behavior,' though behavioral issues can impact sleep. Ignoring a baby because they don't sleep isn't going to suddenly get your bundle of joy to just sleep when told to.

Sleep struggles in children are quite different from behavioral issues. Research points out the importance of the connection between sleeping and bonding time with caregivers. When a baby cries before they go to sleep, this connection can be hindered if the parent does not provide the child with the emotional reassurance the baby needs. During the early weeks and months of a child's life, babies rely on their parents to provide them with this comfort and security.

These early times of life are a sensitive time for young babies. When parents implement an outdated method of letting the child cry-it-out before they provide them with comfort, they are increasing the risk of long-term attachment issues or even a lack of attachment. There are a number of reasons why the cry-it-out method, of any variation, causes harm to a young infant. That is why I recommend this be avoided as an approach to sleep training.

For instance, leaving a child to cry-it-out for any length of time increases cortisol levels. They become more and more stressed the more they are left to cry. Even when the parent returns to console their crying child, only to leave and allow them to cry again, the child learns to not trust the parent. I'm aware that there are individuals who would argue against this - that entering the room to console your child without giving them much contact is not damaging. As a parent and professional in baby sleep patterns, I understand fully how this old approach causes a number of issues that are not easily fixed and can lead to more intense issues as the child grows.

Even if there is an improvement in the child's sleep pattern, there are a lot of negative consequences that occur in their developmental, emotional, and mental state of being. A majority of these issues may not come to light until the child is several years older. Some suggest that these techniques are suitable for children over 6 months of age - treating sleep issues, essentially, as behavior problems. We now have a better understanding, however, that the prefrontal cortex and hippo campus are not fully developed until the child is in their adult years. Using a cry-it-out method can hinder these areas from developing properly and the child can make strong negative connections with sleep when they are put through the stress of crying it out alone. Therefore, I don't recommend these methods, no matter what age your baby may be.

Most of the research that has been done to downplay the negative effects of the cry-it-out method is significantly flawed, in my professional opinion. For example, they often state that there is little to no difference in using a cry-it-out method over another gentler sleep method though, most of this research includes misleading information.

Up until the late 1980s, pediatric sleep was not a well-researched area. Even with nearly 25% of young children suffering from some form of sleep disturbances, sleep was not closely looked at in the pediatric health field (Chamberlin, 2004).

When David was born, this was the approach that we quickly jumped into using. At the time, I had a very different view of what baby sleep was supposed to be like. The cry-it-out method was the only method being discussed and, therefore, it was all we knew to try. For me, seeing my child struggling so much to get to sleep, and hearing him scream for help, was not something I could just ignore. My maternal instincts took over within the first 20 minutes and I rushed in to reassure little Davey that he was safe and that I was there. My knowledge of how stress impairs sleep supported my maternal instincts and my decision to stop using this method. Just one night trying to force this method on my son made me realize there was no possible way I could, with a clear conscience, recommend another parent jump into this method.

In today's modern world there are a lot more factors to consider when it comes to proper sleep, for both infants and adults. The world is a busy place and we now have a much more in-depth understanding of what a young child needs to be able to fall asleep. This isn't helpful for all babies.

In fact, what many parents fear as unhealthy or problems in their baby sleep patterns are actually typical behaviors. Many parents feel they have a "bad" sleeper because their baby wakes frequently throughout the night. While these can be frustrating occurrences and can cause mom or dad to lose sleep, these are actually common sleeping patterns for most babies. This is the most common problem I run into when I begin working with families. They have been made to believe that their baby should be sleeping for longer stretches of time and never wake. Middle of the night wakings are common.

Think about how many times you yourself tend to

wake in the night to change positions or because you're thirsty. Your baby is not any different. When I point this out to new parents, they instantly realize that they have been setting the bar too high for their little one. They can then address the real issues their baby is struggling with. Nearly 9 out of 10 families that I have worked with have simply not given their baby the opportunity to learn how to fall back asleep on their own.

There is no one-size-fits-all method. There is no magic bullet that will get a child to fall asleep and stay asleep, without a few tears or a little resistance. We can combine all the theories and methods and still they may not work. What parents need to realize is that it is not the number of techniques you use, it is simply finding and sticking to the right method for your own unique baby.

In the past, sleep training was approached in a way where the parent would be encouraged to ignore or wean the baby off of their successful sleeping tools.

Parents were told to be structured and strict with getting their young baby to follow a sleeping routine that was more 'enforced' on them as opposed to teaching. What results from this approach is a great deal of resistance and stress for the baby and parents.

Recent findings, and in-depth research, have discovered that a gentler approach to sleep training is not only beneficial for babies but for mom and dad as well. Getting your baby to sleep better is not just about their health and wellness. The mental health of the caregiver's needs to be taken into account too. When mom and dad are sleep-deprived, they are unable to properly care for their child. How does one tackle these many concerns with confidence and less struggle? It comes from first understanding our baby's natural sleep process. Then, we work with that process to create a specific plan that promotes and encourages your little one to fall asleep with no fuss and no crying.

The Nature of Sleep

Sleep is a complex process that many of us take for granted. For your baby, sleep is a time to process and organize all the new information they encounter throughout the day. For older babies, this is a time for their immune system to strengthen and cells to grow. As your baby grows, their sleep patterns will change and their routines will need to be adjusted in order to promote proper development. New parents tend to have this idea that their baby, at some point, is going to sleep undisturbed through the night. But, as you know now, it's quite common for babies to wake up a few times at night and then fall back to sleep. This is no different than how adults sleep. Sleep is rarely unbroken.

When we take the time to truly understand the sleep process, we can relieve ourselves of unnecessary stress and the unattainable expectations that we place on our baby when it comes to sleep. We've talked about this briefly but let's look a little deeper.

Sleep Process Components

Adults and babies go through a certain process when it comes to sleep. The components that make up this process contributes to healthy sleep and behaviors.

Circadian rhythm - Circadian rhythm is the internal setting our body runs on, and is sometimes also known as our biological clock. This rhythm includes physical, mental, and behavioral changes that we cycle through the day. It is what signals us when it is time to sleep and what allows us to wake naturally on our own. Light plays a crucial part in regulating our circadian rhythm. Natural sunlight lets our body know it is time to get up. Just as closing the currents in, the evening signals the brain to start releasing melatonin to prepare for nighttime sleep. There are a number of factors, apart from light exposure, that can affect our circadian rhythm. These factors are divided into specific categories such as biological mechanisms, environmental factors, lifestyle habits, and homeostasis. Examples of these factors include:

- Melatonin levels
- Cortisol levels
- Eating habits
- Body temperature
- Blood pressure
- The digestive system

A baby's circadian rhythm begins to emerge within their first 4-6 weeks of life. It will not fully develop until they are at least three-months-old.

Sleep associations - These are what trigger us to know when it is time to sleep. Most of these are external factors like a dark and quiet environment. Many newborns begin to associate feeding with sleep as they tend to drift to sleep while feeding. Other factors are swaddling and pacifiers. Babies that are over 6 months old may begin to sleep with a special blanket or stuffed animal. Your baby begins to make these associations after just a few weeks. While these are useful tools to help one get to sleep, many can become a hindrance. If we rely on these too heavily, our baby will need them to fall back asleep when they

Sleep disruptions - Sleep disruptions are internal or external things that cause us to wake from sleep or that keep us from being able to fall asleep.

Sleep latency - Sleep latency is the time in which it takes for one to go from being awake to falling asleep. This time period can indicate when there are indications of sleep deprivation and if adjustments need to be made to the sleep routine. If a child takes less than five minutes to fall asleep, there may be severe sleep deprivation. The ideal time in this in-between wakeful and drifting to sleep stage is around 20 minutes. Anything longer than 20 minutes can be an indication of other concerns.

Sleep pressure/sleep drive - This is the biological timing of when we feel more pressure to sleep. We subconsciously feel more tired and, if we try to sleep outside of this time, we are often left lying awake. This causes one to become even more unsettled. Your little one goes through this as well. When they are feeling tired, they need to sleep. Knowing the ideal time to encourage your little one to sleep will result in a much smoother sleep transition and a happier and healthier baby and parents.

Sleep stage/cycle - For adults, there are four sleep cycles, three of which are spent in NREM and one in REM as we previously discussed. The length you spend in each cycle varies, and most adults will cycle through these stages, multiple times. Each time the length they spend in REM sleep tends to increase.

In stages one and two, we are in NREM sleep. We can be easily awoken and are often quite calm if woken up. Many of us experience hypnotic jerks and our thoughts tend to be clear and consistent during this time. Adults tend to spend a great deal of their sleeping time in these stages, whereas babies and younger children need to spend less time in these stages.

We then move onto stages three and four where we enter into restorative sleep. This is where our body heals itself, cells grow, there is an increase in blood flow to muscles and our breathing is slower as our blood pressure drops. In these two stages, we are in deep and slow sleep so we are not easily awoken. We are unaware of what is occurring around us. In these stages, night terrors can occur, sleepwalking is more common, and we may also grind our teeth. For children, this is the stage of sleep where bed wetting also occurs. As your baby grows, there is less time spent in these two stages.

The final stage of the sleep cycle is REM sleep. During this stage, we are organizing our memory and transitioning our experiences from short-term memory to long-term memory. This is the stage where babies begin to form nurturing connections with what they have experienced through the day. During REM sleep, one can be easily woken. The body will be immobile and completely relaxed at this time. This stage is also when we might experience nightmares.

Unlike adults, babies tend to fall right into their

REM sleep or active sleep. They spend half their time asleep in this active state and the other half of their time in NREM3 or quiet/slow-wave sleep. This sleep cycle tends to remain until they are about 3-months-old, when they will begin transitioning to the typical four-stage sleep cycle. Adults run through three different stages of NREM sleep before reaching REM sleep; this full cycle tends to take about 90 minutes for adults. Throughout the night, most people will cycle through these sleep stages multiple times. A baby tends to only have a sleep cycle that lasts about 50 minutes before they wake and fall back asleep.

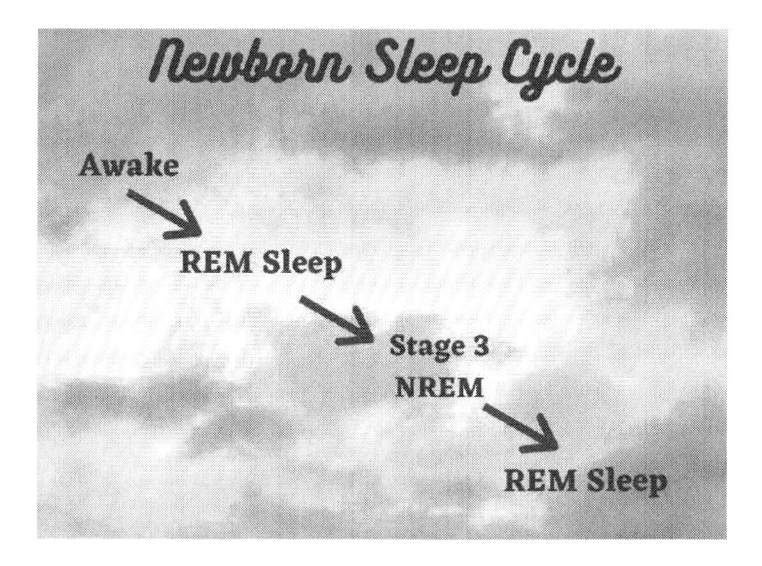

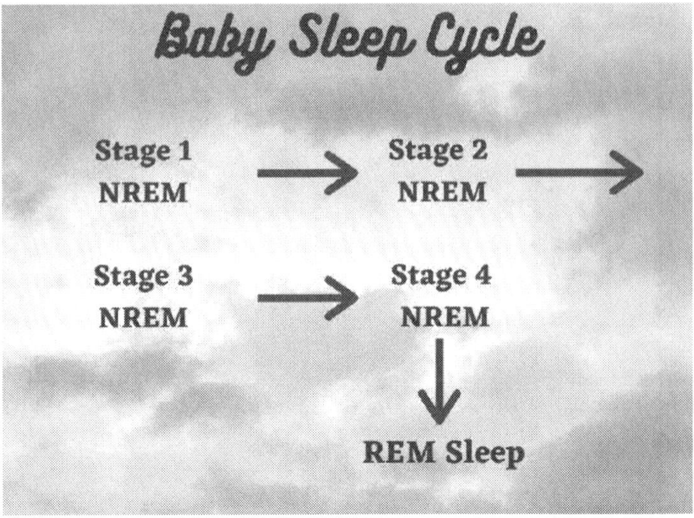

Baby Sleep Cycle

Stage 1 NREM → Stage 2 NREM →

Stage 3 NREM → Stage 4 NREM

↓

REM Sleep

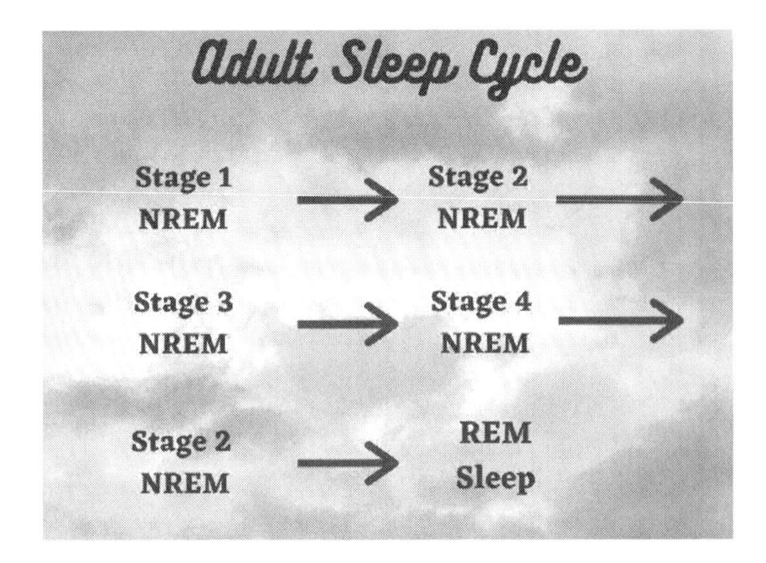

REM and NREM sleep cycles are vital for proper rest and development. As we grow older, our need to enter into REM sleep diminishes, but this doesn't occur for many years. We first need to transition and gradually become more accustomed to falling into the different stages of NREM sleep and spend less time in REM sleep. Sleep cycles for babies under three months tend to be simple and straightforward. They enter into REM sleep, transition to NREM sleep stage three and four, then go back into REM sleep. They are often not spending much if any time in the first two NREM stages of sleep. As they reach the three-month milestone, these stage one and two NREM cycles come into play.

Which Kind of Care Matters Most?

During the earliest stages of life, touch is a vital form of communication for babies. Gently holding and rocking your baby when they are falling asleep, feeling distressed, or when the baby is ill lets them know that they are safe. It gives them the comfort and security they need to remain calm and relaxed even when they are feeling uncomfortable and uncertain. Human contact, and especially the skin-to-skin contact with a baby, begins the bonding moment for baby and parents. This skin-to-skin contact has been highly regarded as being able to calm even the fussiest of babies and ultimately leads to more secure and happier children.

Parental contact fulfills a number of your baby's needs. It helps them feel comfort, security, love, relaxation, and provides them with stimulation. For these reasons, and many others, it is essential that your baby receive plenty of nurturing contact in their first weeks and months.

Many refer to this type of parenting as attachment parenting, which tends to support responding to a baby's needs with sensitivity and kindness. Creating a loving and warm environment for babies to thrive in is a necessity for the proper development of a young child. The environment greatly impacts their ability to sleep soundly in the earliest weeks and months of their lives.

When we replace our anxiety and any worries that we have about our baby's sleep with simply providing them the contact, love, and the emotional connection they need, sleep feels more natural. The process is more enjoyable, and both parents and baby have more success accomplishing their ultimate goal of a more restful sleep.

Choosing a sleep training method will ultimately determine your success. If you keep in mind that babies need more nurturing care and less rigid guidelines, you will find the method that seems like the perfect match for your baby, you, and your entire family. In the next chapter, I'll outline a number of sleep methods that I and others have used with (and without) long-term success.

CHAPTER 2:

BABY SLEEP: METHODOLOGY AND APPROACHES

We just don't know what to do. We know Landon should be sleeping for longer stretches, but every time he starts to squirm, the screaming comes shortly after. I can't just let him cry. I rush in to hold him until he falls back asleep. He is up again within the hour so I try to feed him thinking that's the problem but he barely eats much. This continues throughout the evening. I'm desperate for him to sleep longer, but there has to be some other way than just letting him cry. - Christen.

There are a number of sleep methods parents can try that don't involve high levels of stress or tears, like

Christen is experiencing. As you try new methods to help your baby get to sleep, I have to emphasize that it's critical to stick with one method for at least one week, consistently. Two weeks is even better. It can take a few days for your baby to adjust to all the newness of sleeping in their own crib or in their own room, for example. This is not an adjustment that can be easily made overnight though some parents are lucky enough to experience this. How parents approach this process from the very beginning will make bedtime either more enjoyable or more stressful as your baby grows.

"Old School" Versus Modern Methodology

Now that you have a better knowledge on the sleep cycles of infants and very young children, I think you'll see how and why some methods will work better than others. Keep in mind as well that every child is different. What worked for David when he was a baby, may not work for your little one. What works for your baby, may not work for your sister's child. Sleep training comes in many shapes and forms. Many parents rarely find that a single method or approach to getting their little one to sleep through the night works on the first try. So, be patient with yourself and with your baby.

Fading method

This method is best for babies between the ages of six to eight weeks. You subtly begin to wean off the typical methods you have used to get your baby to sleep. Rocking them to sleep or feeding them just before bedtime will be done in shorter periods of time. They are able to learn self-soothing skills for falling back to sleep. This method minimizes the crying that tends to come along with teaching baby sleeping habits as it doesn't completely eliminate what has worked in the past.

Pick-up/Put-down method

This is another minimal-cry approach to sleeping. Babies from six to eight weeks can begin to associate being laid down in their crib with sleeping time. This involves you holding your baby until they are no longer fussy or crying. Once calm, place them in their crib. If they become agitated again, pick them up to provide solace until they are settled, then put them back in their crib. This process is repeated until your little one falls asleep. This is a great way to reassure and comfort your baby through a gentle, consistent technique. The success of this technique, however, completely depends on your child's personality.

This is one of the favored methods for those wanting to transition their baby to more independent sleep. One family I worked with, for instance, called me to help them get their extra-fussy little one to stay asleep for longer. After determining that their baby was developmentally ready to sleep for longer on their own, we went over what they had been doing.

Basically, they were implementing the pick-up and put-down method with no luck, for a little over a month. They were set on using this approach because they wanted to provide their child with extra cuddles to help ease them to sleep. I observed them using this approach and could easily see that each time they picked up their child and placed them back down, the baby became even more enraged then before. The child's screaming became louder and more high-pitched. This clearly wasn't working.

I recommended they try a slightly different approach. My suggestion is holding their child a little longer until they almost fall asleep, instead of just until the baby calms down. It seemed to me that laying their baby down, while it was still relatively alert, scared and upset the child even more. Waiting a little longer, allowed their infant to fall asleep, much more quickly. Had they been strictly set on implementing this method exactly as it 'should' be done, they would have had many more months of sleep struggles.

This method can ease children into independent sleep but should only be used with older babies who are sleeping or transitioning to sleep in their own rooms.

Chair method

This is a common method used for older children - above eight-months-old. This works very well for children who are having a great deal of anxiety when it comes to sleeping alone in their own beds. When this strategy is implemented properly, it allows the child to become more familiar and comfortable with their sleep environments. They become more relaxed being in their own room with a parent. After which, they gradually learn to feel safe and secure, even when the parent is a slightly farther away. This method also addresses attachment issues and slowly allows the child to be okay with the parent not being in the same room with them. The chair method is helpful when your older baby wakes in the middle of the night and screams when mom or dad is not in sight. It teaches them to soothe themselves back to sleep without needing an adult in the same room.

Children who are used to co-sleeping with parents, or who have made it a habit to scream for their parents in the middle of the night, need to learn that they are safe in their own rooms and that mom and dad are still in the same house. When you begin this method, you will first begin by setting up a bed for mom or dad next to the child's bed. For the first week, you will sleep next to your child and, if they startle in the middle of the night, gently pat them until they fall back to sleep. This allows your child to know that you are still there and within reach.

For the next week, you will sleep in the same room but try to avoid any physical touch when your child wakes in the middle of the night. During the second week or starting in the third week, you will remove your temporary bed from your child's room and instead place a chair in its place. The chair should be arm's reach away from where your child is sleeping. This allows you to give your child the reassurance they need when they wake up in the middle of the night. As your child gets more used to falling to sleep on their own, as long as you are present, you will begin to slowly move the chair further away from the bed when it is bedtime. This process can take up to a few weeks to complete; by then, you will have removed the chair and your child should be able to drift off to sleep as you are walking out of the room.

This can be a tricky method to implement since many children may think that mom and dad are just playing a game with them. To avoid getting your child overly excited in the process, as you sit in the chair or lay next to the bed, keep your eyes closed. Most children will mimic their parents, so this encourages them and reinforces that it is time for bed.

Keep in mind that if this method is used during a developmental milestone, or while the child is teething, it can take longer for this approach to work. Also, work with your child when using this method. If your child is not ready for you to be sitting next to the door at bedtime, move the chair back up a little. You don't want to force this method on your child. You want to keep the trust and sense of security your child has when you are in the room, but you also want them to utilize what they know when it comes to going to sleep and call on their own self-soothing methods for bedtime.

Concerns with Sleep Training Methods

The main issue with a number of sleep training methods is that they encourage parents to ignore their baby's cues when they need something. They often neglect to teach parents that their baby has specific ways of crying to communicate what they need. Instead, parents are often told to let their baby soothe themselves, most often by crying it out. There are many long and short-term negative effects these cry-it-out methods can have. As I've mentioned, and experienced, they can take a toll on the baby's own development and can hinder the bond and security they feel in their own sleep environment.

When parents gain the understanding that their baby sleep struggles aren't really struggles at all but are typical of their age and development, there is less stress and expectation placed on the baby. Parents are then able to approach their child with more love and comfort instead of distress and hopelessness when it comes to bedtimes and naps.

More modern approaches to sleep training involve taking the baby's individual personality, temperament, and needs into consideration. We'll continue to explore this but first let's look at how feeding and sleeping behavior can be connected in a healthy way.

Connecting Feeding to Sleeping Behavior Training

Feeding a newborn is a nurturing and bonding experience for parents and baby. It is a time that should not be filled with stress and anxiety. Unfortunately, this is often the case for many new parents, who worry whether their baby is eating enough, crying too much, burping sufficiently, and so on. First time parents second guess whether they are simply doing enough to ensure their baby is healthy and happy. A majority of babies who have issues with feeding, whether breastfed or bottle-fed, will have sleeping struggles as well.

Newborns will often sleep most of the day waking usually just to eat or fuss about a dirty diaper for the first few weeks. After that, they will often begin to stay awake for a limited amount of time, but will often sleep shortly after or while being fed. For the first month or two, babies need to eat frequently and it is best to let your little one lead the schedule.

Feeding on-demand ensures your baby is eating the right amount for them. It also ensures that those who are breastfeeding will build up an appropriate supply of milk for the baby.

Tracking our baby's natural sleep and eating cycle will allow you to create a specific sleeping schedule that caters to their own internal clockwork. Knowing when our newborn typically feels hungry and tired prepares us to teach them proper sleeping habits. Most parents do allow their infant to form an association with feeding and then sleep. This is not wrong. I have encouraged many new parents who have a newborn to feed, then place their baby down to sleep, as this is what many newborns tend to do naturally. Down the road, however, this tends to be the most common nighttime struggle encountered.

Eventually, your baby will not need as frequent feedings through the night but, every time they wake, you feed them to get them to return to sleep.

This is how many parents get their child to sleep and is a convenient way to quickly get your little one back to sleep. The problem is, however, that every time your baby wakes up in the night, they have learned to expect a feeding. They don't know any other way to go back to sleep on their own because they haven't been taught to do so.

Tracking Feeding and Sleep

	Time						
Feed							
Sleep							
Awake							
Diaper Change							

We can begin to disconnect the feeding/sleep association by keeping our baby awake when offering the breast or bottle. Once they are finished, place them into bed as their eyes start to shut. We want babies to be full, happy and drowsy, not completely asleep when they are placed in the crib. When we place our baby into bed after they fully dozed off, their last memory is you holding them. When they awake in the middle of the night, no longer in your arms, they will be confused and afraid because this is not how they recall falling asleep. This is where sleep coaching comes into consideration. We begin to identify what is causing our baby to wake in the night or what struggles they are having with sleep and address the root of the problems. We don't make assumptions, but learn to listen to the needs of our baby and work with them to form healthy sleep habits.

Sleep Coaching

While old school methods have clear cut instructions and directions for parents to follow, gentler approaches require more assessments and a holistic approach to baby sleep cycles. Each process includes taking into consideration distinct factors that impact sleep and integrate this knowledge with your baby's specific temperament.

Sleep coaching, or sleep training, is how we teach our little ones to fall asleep on their own. Your baby learns to fall asleep without the need to be rocked, fed, or snuggled, and is able to quickly fall back asleep when they wake up suddenly in the middle of the night. This ensures your baby is getting the right amount of sleep each day and night. This doesn't have to be a time of stress for baby or mom and dad. Instead, it can be a time to provide your baby with additional comfort and encouragement as they gain a little bit of independence. How one approaches this process is completely up to them. However, research has shown that some approaches can be damaging to the bond that the baby forms with their parents.

The *sleep learning independent plan* and *sleep with assistance plan* are two effective ways that tend to have fewer tears and more success in sleep training a baby. These two approaches take into consideration a number of aspects that can impact your baby's sleep cycle and allow you to create a plan that specifically caters to them as an individual. They include a number of bonding and attachment solutions that can help encourage babies to sleep and makes them feel safe and secure to sleep for longer periods of time.

With sleep coaching, you are providing your baby with new techniques so they can sleep on their own. For the first few months, you have used some vital tools to ensure your little one has slept soundly but they will soon be shifting their sleep cycle and these initial techniques can either be ineffective or cause more issues with sleep as they keep growing.

Sleep coaching encourages:

- Building stronger connections between baby and caregiver.

- Mom and dad to better understand their baby's unique personality and needs.
- Multiple methods to include more physical contact, responsiveness, and compassionate - and realistic sleep boundaries.
- Child and parental confidence.
- Addressing the caregivers' emotional health.
- Using different methods to teach toddlers and infants the importance of sleep through play activities.
- Parents and children try new strategies for addressing developmental phases that impact sleep.
- Teaching parents how to be respectful of their child's individuality and understand what their child's behaviors are telling them.
- Confronting any issues that can lead to poor development of the child.

This method of sleep training gives parents the confidence and reassurance that they are taking a proactive part in teaching their infant how to fall asleep in a relaxed and calm environment.

Sleep with Assistance Plan (SWAP)

Sleep with assistance refers to a form of sleep training where the caregivers provide assistance to their baby to help them sleep. They begin to introduce a consistent routine around sleep that will help the baby better identify the difference between awake and playtime versus sleep and quiet time.

This plan begins by setting a solid foundation for sleep and builds from that foundation. Simple guidelines for accomplishing this plan include:

1. Create a bedtime routine.
2. Being consistent with a bedtime that is age appropriate.
3. Consistent calming activities done before bedtime.
4. Creating a proper sleep environment.

SWAP gradually encourages your baby to sleep independently. This method can be implemented in the first few weeks after your baby is home; you can go through different bedtime activities to see which ones work best for you and your little one.

When expecting parents come to me for advice on what they can do to get their newborn to sleep through the night on the first day, I tell them that's an impossible goal. One family was very adamant on how important it was for their baby to sleep through the night as soon as possible because of the demanding jobs both mom and dad had. Mom would be working from home for the first three months after their little one was home, and then would be returning to the office. Dad had to be up early to get to his job on time and would return around 6 pm during the week.

I understand why many working parents are eager to get their little one to sleep through the night, and they are not wrong for wanting this. I, however, always tell these parents that they are setting themselves up for more frustration when they have this expectation or goal in mind too soon. With this family, we were able to formulate a plan that would ease their baby into sleeping on their own when the baby was ready. I reminded them that when their baby is ready may not align with when they want their baby to be ready.

We established a calm bedtime routine that both mom and dad participated in as soon as the baby got home. They had a plan in place for when they would like their child to go to bed and wake in the morning, so mom would have more than enough time to get ready for work in the morning. We discussed issues they may encounter and how they could approach these with patience and understanding. We identified which routines would change over time as a result of their baby not needing to be fed in the middle of the night and how to go about handling these late-night awakenings.

They were able to implement their bedtime schedule and waking schedule with more ease because of the routines they had already been practicing from day one. They had already been teaching their baby that night was for sleep and the day was for being awake. They taught their child, early on, that there are a number of calming activities before bedtime so that the baby would naturally relax and get drowsy.

The SWAP method makes small changes in assisting your baby to fall asleep. While it is considered a gradual approach, most babies adjust to these minor changes relatively quickly. As I've said multiple times, it really does depend on your baby's individual temperament. Some of the techniques used in the SWAP plan can include:

- **Sleep shaping** - This technique focuses on lengthening the amount of time your newborn baby sleeps for. This sleep training tool usually starts after the baby has been home for four weeks. This lets the babies begin to regulate their own sleep patterns and understand their internal feeding schedule. Basically, parents resettle their baby back into sleep when they wake or stir in the middle of the night by patting and shushing them. If the baby goes back to sleep, then they do not need to be fed. What they need is a little coaching to nod off once more. If the baby begins to fuss and exhibit discomfort, then this is an indication that they need to be fed. What is so great about using this technique is that there is zero expectation that your baby will go back to sleep. Since it is typical for your baby to wake up occasionally, parents can simply use this as a starting point to teach their baby they don't need to cry in order to fall back asleep.

- **Multisensory strategies** - This is a tool that a number of parents already use without realizing it. Multisensory strategies take into account the setting and environment when they are putting their baby to sleep. For instance, how much light and noise is the baby exposed to when they are sleeping? Are you using a swaddle to comfort your baby to sleep? Is the air stagnant or fresh? These all play a role in proper sleep patterns for babies. Sleep coaching addresses them all to create the perfect environment for ample shut-eye. More on this later!

- **Seated settling techniques** - This is fairly similar to the fading method discussed previously. You slowly begin to lessen your involvement in the sleep process until eventually your baby is calmly able to fall asleep on their own, with no tears. This will encourage them to fall back to sleep when they wake in the middle of the night.
- **Gentle behavior modification** - The tools that you choose to use while sleep training will typically focus on changing one sleep behavior or subbing in a new approach. A gentle modification of your baby's sleep process requires you to identify the patterns in your baby's sleep to determine whether

sleep training is necessary. There are a number of factors that contribute to sleep disturbances in babies and most of these do not require interference from the parent. If a pattern persists for more than a week, beginning a gentle approach to modify the behavioral issue that may be interrupting your baby's sleep might be the best choice you make.

- **Rubber band** - This is a technique that can work really well with toddlers and older children who tend to make their way into your bed or bedroom during the night. If this is something that is disrupting your sleep, the rubber band approach can help eliminate their late-night visits. Whenever your child makes their way out of their bed and you wake up to find them getting comfortable in your room, you quietly and calmly lead them back to their own bed. In other words, the "rubber band" stretches as they go into your room, and you bring it back by bringing your child back to his or her room.

While many parents are attracted to this approach because of the gradual succession of making changes to their baby's sleeping habits, it can take weeks for the new adjustments to become a habit for your little one. You will need to be committed to making the changes, consistently, and it will require a great deal of patience.

How to do it:

The SWAP method can be used to gradually wean babies from their newborn sleeping tools and to introduce more independent sleeping tools. Keep in mind that giving your baby plenty of cuddles and contact in the first few months builds a strong bond between you and your baby. So, you don't want to begin implementing this method until it is age-appropriate; most often this is not until around the three or four-month mark. Rocking and cuddling your baby are often the first sleep associations your baby forms since they are already used to this from being in the womb. However, there comes a time when this isn't idealistic for parents who need to get sleep as well.

This constant need for rocking and cuddling to remain asleep also ultimately disturbs their sleep. When they wake in the middle of the night, they begin to expect these cuddles to help them fall back asleep which means they are missing out on plenty of sleep they could be getting if only they knew how to drift back to sleep on their own. Let's take a look at how you would implement the SWAP method to teach your baby to sleep without these constant comforts:

1. If you want to wean your baby off having to be held close to you while they sleep, you will begin by introducing a little space between the two of you during your bedtime routine. This means, instead of holding your baby tightly next to your body, you will lay next to

them (once they have almost fallen asleep, you move them into their own crib). Lay next to them maintaining a little space between the two of you. Your little one may try to nudge their way back to you, in which case you will comfort them and then move a little bit away from them. It is very likely that they will continue to move closer. When this happens, place your hand on them and tap gently until they fall asleep. You will continue with this routine of lying next to them, with a little space between the two of you, for a week.

2. After a week of a little space, you will increase the space between you and your baby. Now there may be six inches or more space between the two of you which can cause your baby to be a little uncomfortable. Place your hand on them and softly sing or hum to them as they drift to sleep. Maintain this pattern for a few days, being consistent to keep at least

six to twelve inches between you and your baby during your nighttime bed routine.

3. The next step increases the distance so that you are about an arm's length away. You place your hand on their belly and hum, or sing them to sleep. At this point, your little one may be getting used to not having to be so close to you and will be falling asleep much faster on their own. Keep in mind that there are still going to be frequent wakings in the middle of the night when you may need to hum and place your hand on the baby to get them back to sleep. Don't lose hope. While you may be thinking this isn't working, be consistent, and move onto the fourth step.
4. At this step, you maintain an arm's length distance from your baby; you may even begin to place them in their own crib instead of having to move them once they have almost fallen asleep. Keep your hand on their belly

and continue to hum and sing them to sleep. At this step, however, you will begin to decrease how long you hum or vocally coax them to sleep. You will want to sing or hum for only three to five minutes, then close your eyes and pretend to be sleeping as well. Baby's love to mimic their parents so this is incredibly encouraging for them. Your little one may be resistant and still be awake but keep your eyes closed. If needed, hum again, with your hand still on their stomach, and then pretend to be asleep again.

5. As your baby takes less and less time to fall asleep, you can begin to remove your hand from their stomach. Hold it there when you first place your baby into their crib and hum or sing a song or two, then slowly remove your hand and close your eyes as if you are sleeping. Your baby might be fussy during this time. After a few minutes, if your baby is still fussing, place your hand back on their

stomach, hum another song, then slowly remove your hand. Pretend to be asleep once more. Continue this process, shortening the time you leave your hand on their stomach until they are fully asleep.

6. Now you can begin to place the baby into their crib without having to place your hand on their stomach. Continue to hum or sing a song or two at first, then close your eyes and pretend to sleep. During this step, your baby will probably feel secure and safe enough in their crib after the first day or two and they will fall asleep after a few minutes of you singing.

While the process is simple enough, many parents give up too soon when they are still struggling to get their baby to sleep through the night. As we will cover later, there are certain expectations that parents have when it comes to their baby's nighttime sleeping that are simply just myths. This method helps you make progress in extending your baby's sleep and ensures that they are getting the quality and quantity of sleep they need. The key thing to remember is that it will take at least five to seven days for your little one to master their new sleeping skills, or sleeping without their parent's constant presence. How do you know if you are making any progress?

- Bedtime won't feel like a torturous chore. You and your baby will begin to enjoy your bedtime routines together, even if you may struggle a few nights to stay on track.
- Your baby is actually sleeping longer. Even when it seems as though your baby is waking just as much as they were before, tracking their bedtime time and wakings will help you see the real picture of the progress that is being made.
- You have transitioned your baby to a more permanent sleeping environment, like their own room or in their own crib.

- You have seen enough improvements in their nighttime sleeping that you can start implementing the same strategies for their nap time routine.
- Your baby is at the right age to begin shifting to a more permanent and longer sleep/feeding schedule. One where they won't have to wake up as frequently during the night to be fed.

You may not be saying yes to all of these things but even saying yes to a few can mean you are on the right track. Some of these methods may not be suitable for your baby and they may not be ready to sleep fully on their own. If you have been consistent with the process for a week or two, and haven't seen any progress, it might be time to reconsider your approach. Shifting your coaching method is never an easy decision but in some instances it is necessary. In Chapter 10, we go into further details about when you should change your coaching method and how to do this successfully.

Sleep Learning Independent Plan (SLIP)

This is another method that encourages your baby to self-soothe and learn to fall back asleep on their own. This is done without the parents needing to come in for reassurance or assurance. Your baby will feel safe enough to fall asleep on their own without having to be rocked, bounced, or fed. You'll create a plan where your baby will learn to fall asleep without the parents interfering. SLIP provides your baby with the opportunity to learn life-long healthy sleep habits; so, this technique is important for developing general sleep health, and I encourage you to try some or all of this plan with your child, especially as they get a little older.

When parents have an older child, this is often an approach I recommend if all other methods have been unsuccessful and there are no additional medical conditions that could be causing issues with sleep (we talk about this later on). If you have already been consistently putting in the effort and time with the SWAP plan, and are still on the struggle bus with your baby sleeping, then SLIP can be the answer to your baby's sleeping needs.

This approach is often used when families are struggling with severe sleep deprivation. Families turn to this plan when their baby has formed very strong sleep associations that have been strengthened over months, and for older children, years. With a strong commitment to the process, however, many parents find success with this approach in just a few days. It is, however, just as normal to take a few weeks for your little one to adapt to the changes in sleep expectations.

The downfall of this approach is that some tears will be shed by your little one. This isn't to say that you will just leave your child to cry and figure it out on their own. It will be a new experience for them and some babies are not skilled at handling change with much grace. I say this from experience. While we eventually found a gentle and calm approach with our first son, our second was a bit more headstrong and resistant to change. When you are mindful about your child's sleep cues, you can limit the tears your little one will cry. All the while, you still provide them the comfort they need to learn to sleep independently.

How to do it?

When committing to this plan, you will want to ensure your baby is in a safe sleep environment. Though SLIP can be done while co-sleeping and for transitioning your child into separate bedrooms (we'll get into details about sleep environments later in this chapter), it is more successful and only recommended after your baby has become comfortable with their own sleeping environment.

You will need to dedicate a few weeks of consistency to this approach though many parents find their baby is sleeping better after the first few days of implementing the SLIP method. The key to success is consistency, and this isn't just with the evening routine. Naps are a necessity and you need to ensure that your baby is napping appropriately during the day. This means they are not taking more naps than necessary and the naps are not longer than considered typical for their age. (In Chapter 7, we cover age-by-age daytime and nighttime sleep recommendation.) Naps don't have to be done independently at this point. The focus is to ensure they are happening at the right time to better promote longer evening sleep.

You will want to use sleep words to strengthen the language association when it is bedtime. We used *"night night"* as our sleep words. I know families who have used *sleep tight"* or *"beddie-bye."* Use the same words every night, use them firmly, but in a caring way, so your child understands that playtime is over and it is time for sleep. The bedtime routine needs to already be consistently applied. You will need to have a clear understanding of when your baby typically falls asleep in order for this approach to be effective. Just dabbling with random bedtimes up until now is not recommended. With our second son, Josh, we would begin using our bedtime word in the bedtime routine. We would say:

"It's bath time so we can get ready for night night."

"Let's read a book before night night."

Then when it was time for him to go to sleep, I would tell him that I loved him and "night night."

When it is time for your baby's bedtime, place them in their crib, sing them a song, or read them a book. Give them a kiss and tell them goodnight, or use whatever word you have dedicated to reiterate that it is time for sleep, then leave the room. If they begin to fuss or cry, count slowly to ten before returning. When you enter the room, re-state the sleeping phrase and provide them with a little comfort. This can be picking them up and holding them until they have stopped crying or gently patting or rubbing their back or belly until they have calmed. Then you leave the room again.

If they begin to cry and fuss another time, count

slowly to thirty and repeat the calming process. Continue to increase your wait-time by thirty seconds each time they begin to fuss. If they wake up in the middle of the night, you will want to wait at least a minute before entering the room to comfort them.

There are going to be tears with this approach, and it sounds fairly similar to the cry-it-out approach that gained popularity in the 80s. Rest assured, this is different on a number of levels. First, this is not the go-to approach you want to take. Second, it is only recommended for older children who are at the appropriate age to be sleeping for longer chunks of time in the night without having to be fed. We waited until Josh was a little over a year before deciding we needed to take a little bit firmer approach. Third, you are not just leaving your baby to cry-it-out. You provide them the comfort and love they need at the beginning of the bedtime routine. You have already established they are in a safe and nurturing environment. Fourth, this approach takes careful consideration of your baby's biological clock. You are not just forcing your child to sleep on their own at a time when their bodies are not tired and therefore just leaving them to cry themselves into exhaustion. So, while there will be crying you are not turning to this method as a quick fix.

Environmental Factors

There are plenty of ways that your baby's sleep environment affects their sleep. They have gone from being in a tightly closed space (womb) and now they have all this room and nothing to provide them with security and comfort.

For the first three to six weeks of the baby being home, much of their environment should mimic that of the womb. Contrary to what many parents believe, this doesn't mean that they have to stay in a dark quiet room to be able to sleep. Light exposure, temperature, and sound play a vital role in baby sleep patterns. Each of these components can help set the baby's circadian rhythm, so they wake up and go to sleep at an appropriate hour. Though babies will still need to wake in the evening for feeding until they are at least a year old, a healthy sleep environment will help them go back to sleep faster.

We discuss the sleep environment frequently throughout this book. It is important to set up the right sleeping space for your newborn and make adjustments to this space as they grow. We discuss it thoroughly in Chapters 4 and 6 when we get into safe sleep and why external factors have such a powerful effect on baby’s sleep. Until then, think about the sleeping environment you have for your baby, including temperature and humidity, lighting, sound, and overall comfort. We’ll get into specifics, but you can immediately consider what changes you might want to make in your baby’s sleeping environment.

Weaving Together Grandparents' Wisdom and Breakthrough Findings

Teaching your baby to sleep better addresses the different needs of your child, while also taking into consideration the needs of your family. Typically, parents are either implementing preventive sleep training regimes or therapeutic sleep regimes. Each addresses the specific needs of your baby so you can better ensure they get the rest they need. With preventive regimes, you are setting up a routine to help avoid sleep problems now and in the future. Therapeutic regimes are to help regulate a child's sleep cycle and cope or reduce the issues with already existing sleep problems (we'll get into details about sleeping issues later on).

Our goal is to provide positive sleep associations to our babies so they look at bedtimes and nap time as a relaxing and welcomed part of their day. As early as four-weeks-old, young infants can begin to formulate sleep associations that tend to be linked to sleep. Some of the first sleep associations your baby forms are with classic soothing techniques. These include:

- **Swaddling** - Newborns and young infants love to be swaddled. This is because it is familiar, as they have been used to sleeping in confined spaces in the womb. Swaddling recreates this comforting environment and helps them fall asleep. Many babies, however, fight their parents on being wrapped up in a warm cozy blanket. Many parents forgo swaddling at an early age, even though it is one of the best ways to help soothe a baby to sleep.
- **Side-Soothing** - Not to be confused with side-sleeping, side-soothing is a way you can hold your baby and allow them to calm down and prepare for sleep. A baby should never be placed on their side to sleep, especially newborns. But, holding your baby in a supporting side position as you hold

them and rock them will allow your baby to peacefully drift to sleep. Then you can lay them on their back in a crib once they have fallen asleep.

- **Shushing** - Softly shushing your baby to sleep can help them focus on the sound of your calming voice. This can be used when you have a fussy baby who seems to be distracted by every little noise or movement. Many new parents, therefore, think the best sleep environment for their newborns is one that lacks any noise. However, since babies are used to dealing with a lot of quiet sounds as they sleep, the lack of any noise can actually be distressing for them. A number of babies will then make their own noise by crying.
- **Swinging** - The swinging movement of a rocking crib or safe swing seat can coax your baby to sleep and allow them to stay asleep, while in constant motion. Many new parents learn that if they are holding their baby and

rocking them to sleep in their arms, as soon as they lay them in their own crib the baby awakens and they have to pick them up and rock again. This continues for the duration of the nap or evening sleep routine. Investing in a rocking swing or chair, that can recline fully to a lying position, reduces the need for the parents to rock their child the entire time they are asleep. Ensure that the chair or swing is kept in a safe space where pets or the other adults in the home will not trip over.

- **Sucking** - Babies are used to sucking on their own hands and wrist while in the womb, so it should be no surprise that this can help soothe them to sleep. There is debate over whether a pacifier should be used to help soothe a newborn to sleep. A number of new parents are concerned about having to wean their baby off the pacifier and this can be a challenge. But pacifiers may also reduce the risk of SIDS. You can also teach your child to find their own hand or even thumb to suck on as they are sleeping. This can be helpful when a baby needs this sucking action to lull them back to sleep in the middle of the night.

Most newborns and infants, however, are swaddled and they don't have access to their hands. This is where a pacifier can be useful. This can result in having to enter the room constantly to place it back in your little one's mouth. We struggled with using a pacifier on our first child. Every time it would slip out of his mouth he would scream until it was replaced; then, after just a few minutes, it would fall out again. I'd have to hold it in his mouth until he was back asleep but shortly it would just fall out again. This is when I knew that we had to get rid of the pacifier for him to get a good night's sleep. After a few days of just not giving it to him at the beginning of the bedtime routine, and instead, singing another song and patting him a little longer, he was able to sleep without it.

Understand that these traditional forms of sleep associations are helpful but temporary "fixes." We will eventually need to gradually replace each one with more age-appropriate and independent sleep techniques.

CHAPTER 3:

SLEEPING SCHEDULES FOR A NEWBORN BABY

Little Gabby is an early riser. By early, I mean 4 am on the dot. Every single day, she is up and ready to go. I figured bumping back her bedtime would resolve this issue, but it hasn't. While I wouldn't mind the early rising 4 am is just too early for me to be up and functioning, especially since I've been up late rocking Gabby to sleep. Then she is napping early in the morning when I need to be doing errands or there is a lot going on. I just don't know how to get her to sleep in a little longer before the day begins and this is really making it a challenge to know what I can get done during the day to work around her naps. - Jessica.

Trying to come up with a perfect sleeping schedule for our little ones is no easy task. For most parents, they try to enforce a bedtime that doesn't align with their little one's natural sleep cycle. This is mainly because when we try to correct nighttime sleep issues, we neglect to take into consideration their napping schedules during the day. Additionally, parents rely on their natural instincts to soothe their baby to sleep. Soothing, patting, and other nurturing contact is important for a baby from day one. These are some of the best and effective ways to get a baby to sleep. This, however, poses a problem that almost every parent encounters at some point; all the soothing is causing them, and their baby, to lose even more sleep. Your newborn will need you to get them to sleep but once they have reached the age where their natural sleep cycle begins to kick in, they need to learn new ways to sleep.

Let's take a look at some common problems and how they can be resolved using some gentle sleep techniques.

Bedtime Problems for a Newborn

Deciding when to put your baby to sleep for the night is different for every family. Some feel it is best to put their little one to bed earlier with an earlier morning wake time, for instance from 6 pm to 5 am. Others have more success putting their baby to sleep around 9 pm and allowing them to sleep in until 8 am. What matters most is that your baby is getting enough sleep. Babies who are on a more predictable sleep schedule are more likely to sleep for the appropriate amount of time. However, while some families can easily decide on an early or later bedtime, they may find that sleep issues are still occurring even if their little one is on a consistent schedule. Understand that their bedtime may often be the culprit to their sleeping struggles. It may be necessary for bedtimes to be adjusted, either from later to earlier or earlier to later, to help eliminate the evening sleep issues.

Late Bedtimes

Babies who tend to have a later bedtime often get fewer hours of sleep than those with earlier bedtimes. A later bedtime can be beneficial if your baby tends to wake up in the middle of the night for long periods of time or if your baby is waking up extremely early in the morning, wide awake. Some parents don't mind if their baby is ready to go at 5 am but most would prefer their little one to fall back to sleep for another few hours before they start their day. If your baby is waking up too early, they may be able to sleep in later if their bedtime was moved back to a later time.

If your baby is taking longer than an hour to fall asleep, even though they are giving you signs that they are tired, their bedtime may be too late. If your child is more moody or cranky throughout the day, this is often due to not getting enough sleep through the night. If you feel your baby would benefit better from a later bedtime, you will want to bump back the time you are putting the baby to bed by only 15 minutes at a time. You'll need to stick to this time jump for at least four days before bumping it back another 15 minutes until they are falling asleep and stay asleep better through the night.

As your baby grows, a later bedtime will be more appropriate as they will need less time asleep. This is why it is also important to keep track of how long your baby is sleeping through the night. If your little one is old enough to sleep for long stretches of time, eight to ten hours a night, then a later bedtime of 8 pm will have them waking at around 6 am. This later bedtime works better with your baby's natural sleep cycle and will help you get a little more sleep as well.

Early Bedtimes

Getting started with a bedtime routine earlier in the evening can yield much better results for the baby getting the appropriate amount of sleep. There is often less risk of the baby becoming overtired and resisting sleep. Naps can also give you a clue when your baby is ready to be moved from a later to an earlier bedtime. If your baby is napping for longer than two hours during the day, this can be due to their later bedtime.

Babies over three months of age tend to sleep for longer stretches throughout the night, especially when they are being put down before 9 pm. The problem with this, however, is that many parents find it hard to pinpoint when their baby should get to bed to ensure enough rest in the evening. Many try to force an earlier bedtime on a baby who simply is not tired and therefore will fight against sleeping for an hour or more. To find the right time you will want to begin to bump up their 9 pm or later bedtime by 15 minutes. Stick with the new schedule for a few days before putting them to bed earlier by another 15 minutes. You know you have found the right hour when your baby is falling asleep faster. They will give you signs of sleepiness and they won't wake for long periods in the middle of the night.

Babies who are sleep-deprived tend to skip naps or wake up early but still show signs of tiredness. These babies can benefit from an earlier bedtime to help correct this sleep deprivation. This earlier bedtime isn't always a significant change. For most, it is just 30 minutes earlier than they would typically be put to sleep. Using an earlier bedtime to coax a still tired baby to fall back asleep can be successful only if they have already acquired the self-soothing skills to fall back asleep on their own in the middle of the night.

Napping

Naps are a way to combat the stress response triggered by sleep pressure, or the feeling that we need to go to sleep. When we become fatigued, our body begins to release more cortisol or stress hormones. Naps lower the stress hormones that can make your baby fight going to sleep, even when they are very tired. How naps are scheduled will impact the levels of cortisol in the body. If the baby doesn't nap at an appropriate time, this can cause a buildup of cortisol, which results in the baby being sleep deprived because they simply cannot calm their body down.

When a baby is laid down for a nap too soon, their sleep pressure is not high enough. This is a common mistake parents make when they are trying to figure out the right napping schedule for a baby. They will often try to get their baby to sleep in their awake window instead of their high sleep pressure window. The best approach for scheduling naps is to have them evenly distributed throughout the day.

If you try to get your child to sleep too soon, this increases their sleep latency time. They won't be able to fall asleep quickly and, when they finally do fall asleep, they won't stay asleep for long. This then results in the baby being overly tired later in the day. The opposite is also true. If you wait too long to put your little one down for a nap, their sleep latency is often much shorter. While your little one may sleep for longer during naps, this can impact their nighttime schedule since they won't be ready to sleep again when the evening comes. This causes the baby to go to sleep later which results in not getting enough sleep and then causes the baby to be exhausted the next day. And the cycle continues...

There is no right or wrong approach to the length or number of naps a child takes. Some argue that longer naps will disturb nighttime sleep patterns and throw off the baby's circadian rhythm. Others say that shorter naps do not allow for proper restoration to occur. Both are true for different children. What allows for your child to wake up rested and happy is connected to how you schedule naps. (There are age-appropriate guidelines in Chapter 7.) As your baby grows, the number of naps they take during the day will decrease as well as the time they spend napping.

Developing a consistent sleep schedule takes a bit of trial and error. Let's look at that next.

The Importance of a Sleep Schedule

A predictable and soothing bedtime routine is beneficial for both baby and parents. A sleep schedule takes into consideration the basics of teaching your baby to sleep soundly through the night. By creating a relaxing and enjoyable bedtime routine, you will be promoting better sleep hygiene.

Bedtime Routines

Bedtime routines should include a few calming activities that you will perform each night. This helps the child identify these activities with sleep and makes the bedtime routine more predictable. You are teaching your child the habits they will eventually perform on their own and encouraging a calm and relaxed state for them to fall asleep.

These calming actions can be as simple as dimming the lights and lowering your tone of voice. They can also include listening to calming music, reading a book, soft messages, and baths. For all three of my sons, our newborn bedtime routine was a combination of old-school and modern conveniences. For instance, I would swaddle each of them after they had a nice calming bath. Then I would sing them a lullaby while rocking/swaying them in my arms. I would then sit and feed them as I hummed a song. Once they were done feeding, while I was burping them, I would turn on a white noise machine. When they were just about to drift asleep, I would lay them in their own crib (that was in my room).

A bedtime routine should take about 30 minutes for children over 6 months of age. Babies under 6 months of age will better adapt to a shorter bedtime routine – maybe 10-15 minutes. The key is to be consistent with your evening routine. Ensure that activities remain the same each night – you'll soon notice that your baby will anticipate the next part of the routine and their sleep hygiene habits begin to strengthen.

Sleep Hygiene

Sleep hygiene refers to a child's ability to transition from awake to sleep. Good sleep hygiene also includes setting the right environment to encourage sleep. This can be as simple as ensuring that the sleep environment is clutter and distraction-free, the temperature is comfortable, electronics are turned off, and a bedtime routine is adhered to.

When your baby is getting the appropriate amount and quality of sleep during the night along with their daytime naps, they will be able to fall asleep without trouble or much coaching. Throughout the day, you can help promote appropriate sleep hygiene by keeping them active enough to use up their energy and stimulate them through different forms of physical and educational play.

Understand that good sleep hygiene means your baby will sleep when they are tired; this can mean letting them have an extra 30-minute nap during the day. This teaches your baby that they shouldn't neglect sleeping when they feel they need it. These sleep hygiene lessons you teach your child at an early age will be habits they carry with them into adulthood.

Achieving the Proper Bedtime Schedule

You want to work around your baby's sleep cycle to implement a bedtime routine that they can get used to. Knowing the signs your baby gives you when they are getting sleepy will help you formulate a schedule that results in less struggle, stress, and resistance.

What if your baby isn't getting tired until much later than you would like? There are simple steps that you can take to move up your baby's bedtime as discussed at the beginning of this chapter. This process is made easier when there is already an established and predictable routine in place that lets your baby know it is time for sleeping.

Learning Your Baby's Cues

Learning baby sleep cues, as well as understanding their different cries, will help parents create an effective sleeping schedule. Babies will give you specific clues that they are becoming tired. When these cues first appear, there is often a window of about 15 minutes where your baby will most likely fall asleep without much fuss or resistance.

Signs to look out for:

- Yawning
- Fussiness
- Lack of interest in toys or the people around them
- Turning their face away when being addressed or when you're trying to get their attention
- They will often have a glazed-over expression on their face
- They will begin to wave their arms and legs about

- They may lose some color in their face or have a paler appearance
- They become more and more quiet

Cues your baby is becoming overly tired:

- Making a grimacing face.
- Arching their back.
- They become clingy and will cry to be held and will begin to cry once put down.
- Rubbing their eyes frequently.
- Wiggling about and pulling their knees up to their chest, kicking their legs out.
- They will become inconsolable.
- Pulling on their ears.
- They will rub their face against their caregiver, either against the shoulder or chest of the person who is holding them.

Each baby may exhibit their own number of sleep cues; some may not exhibit any and will seem to jump right into being overly tired. Understanding your baby's non-verbal and verbal sound cues will allow you to better read their body language when they are becoming tired. This can greatly help you know when you should begin running through your evening routine or when the baby needs to be put down for a nap.

The easiest cue to pick up on from a baby is when they begin to turn away from the attention of their parents or caregivers. If your baby is not engaging with you and keeps turning their face away from you, they have probably reached their limit.

Understanding sleep cues doesn't always come easy for all parents. One can begin to better understand their baby cues by reviewing what the typical sleep requirements are for the baby according to its age.

You will notice behavior and mood cues from your child. Children who are not sleeping enough will be more clingy, whiny, and simply miserable throughout the day. Older children may appear to be hyperactive which can cause parents to think they are getting too much sleep. If it is taking you a while to get your child to finally drift off to sleep and they are not staying asleep for very long, they may not need as much sleep as most other children.

Consistent Steps for a Bedtime Schedule

Begin a wind-down time 15 to 3o minutes prior to starting on the actual bedtime routine. This will allow the baby to transition into the bedtime routine with ease. This gives your baby some time to play and have a little more fun after dinner. It also allows them to ease into a more calm and relaxed state. During the wind-down time, you can begin to dim the lights in the home or in the baby's sleeping room, use a calmer and quieter voice, and begin to clean up any toys or distractions.

Simple Bedtime Routine

Wind Down Time 30 minutes prior to bedtime routine
(Dim lights, turn off electronics, use a quiet calm voice)

Bath, Massage, Pajamas 15 minutes

Book or Sing 5 minutes

Feed 10 minutes

Bed Place in crib/bed while still awake but drowsie

Parents should do their best to have plenty of opportunities for quality time with their little one during the day. Some children will often take advantage of the evening as an opportunity to get extra attention if they haven't had enough of it during the day. This is not always easily achieved when both parents are working or there are other little ones that need attention and care in the home as well. There are many ways parents can approach this. You can try to create a more flexible working schedule, or you can cut out some of the activities that keep you booked during the day, so you can focus on bonding with your baby.

CHAPTER 4:

SLEEPING SAFETY: HOW TO DIMINISH THE RISK OF SIDS AND OTHER DANGEROUS FACTORS

I am just so desperate for sleep that sometimes I just let her fall asleep right next to me in bed. When she starts to fuss in the middle of the night, I just move closer and let her latch and she quickly falls back to sleep. I know it isn't really safe, but moving her to and from her own crib every time she needs to feed just wakes her up completely. Then it takes so much longer to get her to fall back asleep and I get less sleep as a result too. There has to be a safer way to feed her without having to interrupt her sleep every time, isn't there? - Lilly.

One of the things I notice about many new parents is that they will do whatever it takes to get the baby to sleep, regardless of safety. Dads end up falling asleep while reclining in a chair holding their little ones, for example, or moms lay on the coach with them and shut their eyes for just a few minutes. In most of these circumstances, no harm results, though, unfortunately, that is not always the case.

It is vital to know everything about SIDS so that you can minimize the risks. Any child under the age of one is at risk of SIDS but ensuring your baby is in the safest and healthiest sleep environment can significantly reduce those risks from occurring. This chapter will review the best and safest sleep choices for your baby. This is a scary topic to discuss but, rest assured, the information provided in this chapter will help you to feel more confident.

What Is SIDS?

Sudden Infant Death Syndrome (SIDS) is the unexplained death of a baby, typically under the age of 12 months. Babies are at the greatest risk between the ages of four to six months. While there is no one agreed-upon cause or factor for a baby to become a victim of SIDS, there is strong evidence that it is due to a developmental delay of the baby's brain. It's believed that there is a delay in the neurological signals that tell the baby to breathe or to wake up when they are struggling to breathe. Parts of the brain that control body temperature, heart rate, and blood pressure may also be underdeveloped which can increase the likelihood of SIDS.

What makes SIDS so devastating is the fact that, in almost all cases, the baby is otherwise completely healthy. Almost all incidents occur while the baby is sleeping, which is why it is often referred to as "crib or cot death." Not all instances where a baby unexpectedly dies in their sleep are SIDS cases. Accidental suffocation and entrapment (where a baby accidentally becomes trapped between two objects, like between the mattress and wall) is another scary, and sadly not uncommon occurrence for babies under the age of one. This, however, is not classified as SIDS. Instead, this falls under the Sudden Unexpected Infant Death (SUID) category. SIDS is a type of SUID but SUIDs include all deaths that occur in babies under one-year-old whether there is a known or unknown cause of death.

Risk factors for SIDS:

- If a baby is put to sleep on their stomach.
- If the baby is put to sleep anywhere besides a crib such as sofas, couch, or an adult bed.
- If the baby is given soft or loose bedding to sleep on or with.
- If they become overheated while sleeping.
- If they are exposed to secondhand smoke, both before and after birth.

- If the baby is allowed to sleep with the family pet like a cat or small dog.
- If the baby shares a bed with a sibling.

How to Diminish the Risk of SIDS

Nowadays, we have a greater understanding of how to reduce the risk of SIDS. The guidelines you put in place as a parent must be followed by all family members or whoever watches your little one, day or night. The best practices to implement to reduce the risk of SIDS include:

- *Back sleeping*

When it was stated in 1992 that babies are safest sleeping on their backs, SIDS cases greatly diminished. Even if your little one fights you on it, it is best to be adamant about your baby sleeping on their back, even for naps.

- *Proper bedding*

Bedding on the crib or cot mattress should be fitted. Your baby should not be able to kick and squirm to loosen the fitted sheet. The mattress should also be flat. You don't want to prop the baby up while they sleep as they lack the head control to lift their head. If it accidentally falls forward the airway may become occluded. You should also avoid placing any objects in the crib; bumpers, blankets, pillows, stuffies, or play toys should be left out of the bed.

- ***Sleepwear***

Babies should be dressed in separate sleepwear for bed. Avoid keeping your baby in loose-fitting clothing for sleeping. Instead, your baby should be put in comfortable sleepwear or a wearable blanket. Babies, two to four-months-old, should be swaddled.

- ***No smoking***

Do not allow anyone to smoke around the baby. Even if someone is not smoking around your baby, they should not be handled by individuals who have just smoked. Cigarette smoke remains trapped in their clothes and on their skin which the baby can then breathe in.

- *Room temperature*

The room temperature is an important factor when it comes to setting up the safest sleep environment for your baby. Many new parents think that the more they bundle up and snuggle their little one the better they will sleep. Unfortunately, this often increases the risk of SIDS. When a baby becomes too hot, they struggle to breathe. This risk is significantly increased when the baby is under six-months-old. Most babies sleep comfortably in a slightly cooler room. To ensure that the room remains at a safe and acceptable temperature, keep an indoor thermometer in the room where your baby sleeps and check that the temperature remains between 65- and 72-degrees Fahrenheit.

Tummy Time

Tummy time is also a daily activity that can help reduce the risk of SIDS. This activity involves placing your baby on their tummy when they are fully awake (someone should always be watching the baby during this time). Tummy time helps babies gain control of their head movement and coordination. It strengthens the neck and shoulder muscles and promotes proper motor skills.

This is also when a child begins to develop the forward curves in their spines known as the secondary curves. When a baby is born, the spine is in the shape of a c-curve. The forward curves in the neck and lower back only develop as the baby lifts her head and starts to crawl, respectively.

Babies should be given the opportunity to have tummy time at least two times a day but three is ideal. When the baby first comes home, it is likely that tummy time sessions will last only a few minutes as they tend to tire quickly. As your little one grows and your baby gains more control, they begin to enjoy this activity for longer periods of time.

Tummy times are best done once your baby has been changed into a clean diaper. You will want to lay out a blanket on the floor and ensure that the area is clear. Sit in front of your baby and encourage them to interact with you as they try to lift their head and move about. This also increases the parental bond with the baby. As your baby grows and the sessions lengthen, incorporate toys into tummy time. Place a toy in front of the baby and watch as they try to reach for it.

Aside from reducing the risk of SIDS, tummy time is also an activity that can help prevent flat spots from forming on the back of your baby's head.

Co-Sleeping

Children under the age of four tend to co-sleep with their parents in one way or another. Even if it is just for one or two nights out of the week, it happens. Our youngest son, Timmy, had a habit of sneaking into our bedroom and setting up all his blankets, pillows, and stuffed animals next to our bed. He did it so quietly that we almost never woke when he was fetching and retrieving all his bedding. We let it go because no one was really losing any sleep over it. He was still happy when he woke up and wasn't sleeping in later because of these nighttime room changes.

Had he been behaving differently or if this behavior occurred more frequently, we would have put a plan in place to ensure he stayed in his own room. If a child's night-time behavior is really impacting the family's sleep, then it is a problem. If parents and child are not suffering from what they think is a sleep issue, it will typically go away and be corrected on its own. We knew that Timmy wouldn't be sneaking into our room when he was older so there was no need for us to make a big deal about it.

Our primarily concern was that Timmy, and our previous children, had the safest sleep environment. For our first, that meant transitioning him into his own room sooner. Our second son needed to stay in the same room with us for longer than we planned.

Our third transitioned well but sometimes needed to feel us nearby. What is safe for one child is not ideal for another.

There are factors that contribute to safe sleeping environments that are not just about what type of bed your baby is sleeping in. While SIDS is known as crib death, it is not the actual crib that increases the risk of SIDS. Instead, it is the sleeping environment that increases the risk. A baby sleeping in their own room, away from parents, is at a greater risk for SIDS because they are further away, and parents remain unaware when their baby may be struggling during their sleep.

Bed sharing is a form of co-sleeping and it can increase the possibilities of the baby accidentally suffocating from blankets or pillows blocking their airways. There have also been cases where a parent may accidentally roll over on the baby. This is more likely to occur if the parent has been drinking or takes medication that can cause drowsiness. This is why it is not recommended that you allow your baby to sleep in the same bed with you. Side-sleepers or side-bed cots can be a safer alternative and can be highly beneficial for those who are breastfeeding.

Safe Sleep Environment

1. Place to sleep on back.

2. Sleep in the same room as parent(s).

3. Tight fitted bedding.

4. Room temperature 65-72 degrees F.

5. Crib away from outlets, electrical cords, blinds,curtains, or any hanging objects.

6. Sleeps in their own crib.

7. Crib is free of toys, blankets, stuffed animals, etc...

8. Sleeps with pacifier.

CHAPTER 5:

FIRST THREE MONTHS: REASONS FOR BAD SLEEP AND HOW TO COPE

We got into a great routine immediately after we brought Shandra home. She was an easy baby. We were able to quickly identify when she needed to be fed, changed, and when she needed to sleep. After the first month though, it all changed. She became extremely fussy throughout the day, and this is making it hard to get her to sleep for longer than 20 minutes at a time. Our easy baby just seemed to do a complete flip, overnight. We haven't discovered any underlying issues for the sudden changes. What are we missing? - Tabitha.

This is a common question that many parents ask themselves. What has caused my loveable and easy-going baby to suddenly fight day and night when it comes to sleep and other activities? For the first three months of your baby's life, they will most likely be calling the shots on how the daily schedule goes. You'll want to feed them when they are hungry, allow them to sleep when they sleep, and spend as much time cuddling, loving, and getting to know your baby. This is a time where parents and babies can deepen and strengthen their bond. Your baby will begin to learn that they can trust you and that they can rely on you to meet their needs. There are very few, if any, sleep coaches that would recommend adhering to a strict sleep plan at this age.

There are infants who struggle with relaxing and being comfortable enough to sleep. If your newborn is resisting sleep, there could be a perfectly good explanation but some may require you to consult a physician for more professional help. This chapter will guide you through the first three months of your newborn's life and what you should know about possible infant sleep disorders that can cause you and baby to lose much-needed sleep.

Causes for Newborn Sleep Problems

Newborn sleep troubles through the first three months can include physical and psychological factors. Babies from birth to three-months-old have a number of adjustments to make. When it comes to sleeping, for example, they lack the ability to distinguish between day and night. Parents can encourage night and day recognition by exposing their newborn to equal time of light and darkness. Newborns are often asleep for a majority of the time and are usually awake to be fed and changed. Most infants at this age are only able to stay awake for one hour at a time before falling back to sleep.

Night feedings occur frequently, often every two to three hours in the first few weeks. Feeding issues can often be the root cause of sleep problems in an infant under six months of age. Since at this age it is highly unlikely that they are not sleeping due to behavioral causes, other areas need to be investigated.

Issues with breastfeeding or bottle-feeding can result in a baby that is hungry. Breastfeeding often improves sleep for both mother and baby. It also decreases the risk of SIDS. Breastfed babies are more easily awoken, which is often why they are less at risk for SIDS than formula-fed babies. If mom is unable to supply enough milk to satisfy the little one, however, the baby may have more trouble sleeping. Many first-time moms are led to believe that breastfeeding leads to more issues with sleep because their baby wakes more frequently in the evening hours to be fed. These wakings are not necessarily interrupting their sleep since they most often are quickly lulled back to sleep while being fed.

Breastfed babies get an additional nutrient, tryptophan, a chemical precursor to melatonin. Since infants do not begin to produce their own melatonin until three to six weeks, this can help regulate the baby's sleep cycle more quickly than formula-fed babies.

Formula-fed babies, however, receive opioid peptides. These can trigger the pleasure response which allows them to quickly fall asleep. Unlike breastfed babies, formula babies can be overfed. This can cause them to be fussy and too uncomfortable to go back to sleep. Overeating tends to be linked to how the baby is fed as opposed to the formula itself. Ways to approach bottle feeding issues include:

- Keep the bottle in a horizontal position.
- Make eye contact with the baby as they are feeding.
- Never prop the bottle up.
- Always hold the baby while feeding.
- Be aware of any stress sign the baby is giving - clenched fist, frowning, dribbling, wide-eyed expressions are cues that your baby is struggling with feeding.

- Never wait for a baby to finish a whole bottle.
- Do not wait until a specific time to give your baby a bottle - give it to them when you see hunger cues.
- Pause frequently while your baby is taking the bottle to allow them to swallow, breathe, and suck.
- Take breaks from giving the bottle to burp the baby.

Normal Sleep Behaviors or Sleep Disorders?

Up until the three-month mark, your attention is going to be focused on building a strong connection and bond with your little one. You want to increase the trust your baby has with you and the other caregivers in the home. This involves responding to your baby's cries and understanding sleep cues.

Newborns will often sleep for 19 hours in total through an entire day (daytime and night). At this age, it should not be expected, or even encouraged, that your child sleep through the night or for long stretches of time. Babies need to be fed frequently since their stomachs are far too small to hold enough food to keep them satisfied for a long time. This means they will be hungrier more often and this is true through the night.

It is completely normal for a newborn to need to be fed at least three times throughout the night during the first few weeks. Neglecting to feed your child frequently at night can result in them not getting enough nutrients and increases the risk of SIDS.

Sleep training is not encouraged at this age. There are, however, things you can begin to implement that will help your baby sleep better:

1. Avoid blue lights from electronic devices; instead utilize yellow or red-toned lights.
2. Avoid heavy play just before your baby is about to sleep.
3. Swaddle your baby.

4. Feed (and always burp) your baby just before sleep time.
5. When your baby needs their diaper changed, if they are or have just fallen asleep, do so in low lighting. Try to only have a small or dim light on so you don't completely wake your baby.

Once your baby is at the two-month mark, you can begin to implement more traditional methods to promote better sleep. You want to avoid sticking to a strict sleeping schedule at this time. You can try out bedtime routines that will help your baby begin to recognize when it is time for longer periods of sleep. Try some bedtime activities such as; giving a bath, rocking in a chair, or reading.

Keep the routine simple and short. If your baby resists these new routines, don't become discouraged. It may simply not be the right time to start new routines; give it a few more weeks and then reintroduce the routines.

Newborn Sleep

(0-3 months)

Total Sleep	Around 19 hours
Duration of each sleep	2-3 hours
Time spent awake between sleeps	Up to 1 hour

**Remember at this age daytime and evening sleeps are almost identical, so the sleep duration tends to be the same.

Sleep Disorders

It is not uncommon for infants and toddlers to suffer through various forms of sleep disorders. Understanding what is actually normal, or typical sleep behavior, will allow you to better identify when there are more serious issues that need to be addressed.

A sleep disorder is one that interferes with the quantity or quality of sleep your baby may be getting. These can be linked to a number of factors such as:

- Developmental delays
- Weight abnormalities
- Obstructive sleep apnea
- Disruptive sleep behaviors
- Restless leg syndrome
- Cataplexy

The most common symptoms of a child or infant who is suffering from an underlying sleep disorder will often:

- Snore in their sleep
- Pause in breathing while they sleep
- Struggle to fall asleep
- Unable to sleep through the night (if they are at the age when sleeping for longer stretches is appropriate).
- Be excessively tired during the day
- Be less active during the day

Plagiocephaly - Better known as flat-head syndrome, occurs when the baby favors sleeping on one side of the head more than the other. This causes the head to flatten. To avoid this, ensure that you adjust your baby's sleeping position so that they sleep on both sides of their head.

Torticollis - When the sternocleidomastoid muscles become tightened or shortened, the baby's head tends to tilt or lean to one side, resulting in torticollis. This can cause babies to feel distressed when sleeping if they attempt to turn their heads in the direction opposite of the way the head naturally leans. This condition also makes it more difficult for babies to feed and this, in turn, disrupts their sleep.

Both plagiocephaly and torticollis can be corrected; both can occur inside the womb, not just as a result of sleeping on one side. Larger babies can suffer from having to squeeze through the mother's pelvis which causes the head to mold and shape into an unnatural position. More often, babies will develop these conditions outside the womb. If a baby is not properly positioned in car seats, swings, or bouncers, for example, their head will begin to slouch to one side.

Babies who are bottle-fed, can develop these conditions if they are placed in a position that causes them to turn their head to the same side during each feeding. Hold babies on alternating sides when giving a bottle, to ensure that they are developing their muscles equally. Skipping on tummy time, previously mentioned, will also cause babies to lack the much-needed muscles to strengthen to support their own heads and gain control over the head and neck movement.

Colic - An inconsolable baby who constantly has a high-pitched severe scream is often suffering from colic. Colic is generally caused, most experts think, by a food intolerance or allergy. Often, a colic reaction tends to subside as the baby gets older and parents can help calm a colicky baby by ensuring they are as comfortable as possible. Rocking, singing, and swaddling can also help with colic.

Gas - Babies are especially sensitive to any trapped gas in their digestive tract causing them to feel abdominal pain, bloating, cramps, and distension. Aside from properly burping, the baby during and after every feeding, parents can massage their baby or place their hands under the baby's feet and gently press their legs up so that the knees go towards the baby's chest. Straighten the legs back out and repeat this a few times to help move gas through their system.

When to See a Pediatrician

Any amount of pain or discomfort can make it impossible for little ones to get proper sleep. Since they are so young, they cannot tell you what is causing them trouble. There are a number of health conditions that can interfere with sleep such as:

- Asthma
- Eczema
- Epilepsy
- Diabetes
- Cancer
- Anemia
- Cystic fibrosis
- Sleep apnea

While symptoms for each condition can vary, children who are suffering from a physical, mental, or psychological condition will exhibit some similar signs.

- Fatigue
- Interrupted sleep
- Emotional dysregulation
- Behavior changes
- Withdrawal from contact or affection

Waiting to see if your baby is just going through sleepless phases can lead to more severe long-term complications. It is best to consult a doctor with any concern you may have in regards to your baby's sleep and overall health.

CHAPTER 6:

BABY SLEEP: THE BASIC REASONS FOR THE MOST COMMON PROBLEMS

We have done everything we can to provide Chance with a quiet sleep environment. When he is sleeping, the phones are turned off, the television doesn't get turned on, and we do our best to avoid going anywhere near the room. Every movement is carefully calculated, so there are no sudden noises he may hear from the bedroom. We can't realistically keep this up though. How do we transition him into his own room and ensure it remains quiet enough for him to sleep soundly? How do we avoid accidentally waking him too early in the morning when we are getting ready for work, or in the evenings when dishes need to be done and work needs to be completed? -Anna and Stephen, first-time parents.

Having the right sleep environment is important for proper baby sleep. A number of new parents want to ensure that it is quiet so their baby will sleep without waking up from sudden noises. Most adults need silence or near silence to sleep soundly, so they think their babies need the same. How much noise is in the baby's room is not the only factor that parents need to be aware of. Parents are often surprised to know how many different influences can affect their baby's sleep and how easy it can be to eliminate these. Becoming aware of these things, results in a baby that sleeps sounder and is healthier.

Around the three to the four-month milestone is one of the best times to begin implementing better sleeping habits. During this time, your baby is able to store information in a more organized manner, such as those connected with sleep time. Up until this time frame, your baby has been taking in a lot of new things from their surroundings and has probably adjusted to being more mobile and entertained. This is also a time when you can more easily break bad sleeping habits that may have been formed over their first four months.

Inner Factors that Affect Sleep

There are a number of internal disturbances that keep your baby from sleeping. These issues are often unavoidable as all babies will suffer from illness, teething, and digestive problems during the course of their life. Most of them are common and can be dealt with relatively easily.

- *Tiredness*

How tired or not tired you baby is will contribute to the difficulties you have putting them to sleep. Excess fatigue causes the body to increase its stress response. As we know, this only adds to sleep difficulties. Your baby is being flooded with cortisol and adrenaline, so their body is amped up even though they are physically and emotionally exhausted. This sets the stage for a vicious cycle. Your baby remains overtired, resulting in more stress hormones being released. What transpires is a situation where it is even more difficult for your baby to settle, calm down, and get to sleep.

It is fairly easy for newborn and younger babies to become overtired. As you know, most newborns can only stay awake for 45-60 minutes at a time. Being up longer than this can cause them to begin to build up their need for more sleep. To get an overtired baby to sleep, we must first get them to relax. If they aren't relaxed, their body is going to just produce the stress hormones that are working against them.

Rocking, holding, and swaddling your baby can provide them with the comfort they need to help them relax. Feeding your baby until they become drowsy is also a good idea. Turn off the lights in their room as you walk around holding them. Have a white noise machine on to encourage them to relax more. Older babies can be read to in a dimly lit room or you can play a calm and quiet activity with them to encourage them to sleep.

Being overly tired is stressful for babies and parents. Remember, your baby will be able to read your signs of stress, too, which makes them feel more uneasy. You want to ensure that you are staying as calm and quiet as possible when you help them get to sleep.

On the other side of the tiredness spectrum is that your baby may not be tired enough to sleep. Where an overtired baby needs to be soothed to be able to get to sleep, an under-tired baby needs more interactions to bring on sleep. Unfortunately, when a baby is under-tired, they give you the same cues as if they are overtired. You will try your best to soothe your baby to get them to calm down and hopefully fall asleep but this is only going to frustrate your baby even more. If you find yourself trying to coax your baby to go to sleep, and you are using all the calming methods you can muster but they are still fighting, it is best to let them play a little longer and then try again.

If this is occurring regularly during the evening bedtime, then you will need to revise their daytime sleeping schedule and see where adjustments can be made so your little one is tired when it is supposed to be bedtime. You also want to see what kind of activities they are doing during the day. You might be struggling with an under-tired baby because they are not getting enough stimulation during the daytime.

- ***Illness***

When a child is sick, sleep can be difficult. This is often true no matter what age they are. Children who have chronic conditions will need to be handled with extra care and precaution to ensure that they are getting the sleep they need. Illness, however, will occur multiple times when your little one is young. This can be minor congestion issues to more alarming fever-induced infections.

Children who have a temperature over 100.4 degrees Fahrenheit are fighting off some form of infection; you should contact your pediatrician for precautionary steps to take. If your child becomes ill, you don't want to deny them the comfort that will help with recovery. You may be rocking, holding, and spending extra time with your little one because that is what they need when they are not feeling well. In these times it is understandable and encouraged that you keep your little one nearby when they sleep. What can occur, however, is the child may expect these sleeping arrangements to continue even after they are feeling better. This can be a real struggle for parents who are caring for a child with chronic conditions. Until they have the long-term symptoms properly managed, either through medication or other means, the child can become used to sleeping in the same bed or room with their parents.

The best way to ease your little one into sleeping alone again, or even for the first time, is using familiar and calming activities. Even if your child is temporarily sick, you should be continuing with a relaxing bedtime routine so they can easily adjust back into their normal routine when they are feeling well.

Parents who have a child with more severe medical conditions, like epilepsy, may be concerned about their child sleeping alone. This is understandable, and until their condition is better managed, it may even be necessary for the child to sleep in the same room as the parents. Once the family has found the right form of treatment to gain control of the seizures, they can begin to transition the child into their own bedroom, if the child is at the appropriate age.

- ***Digestive Problems***

Digestive issues are often identified by tracking your baby's bowel movements. Babies who are formula-fed will often poop at least twice a day and breastfed babies will poop several times a day, usually an hour or two after being fed. When a baby is pooping too much or not enough, this is a clear indication that there is a digestive issue going on that can be adding to or causing sleep problems.

When a baby is constipated, they will often be fussy, especially when being laid down to sleep. It is likely that they are dealing with the same discomfort that you experience when you are having this issue. They are feeling bloated, gassy, and full, so it's no wonder they're having a hard time sleeping. These symptoms often do not become much of a problem unless your baby has gone more than three days without pooping.

If you think that constipation is the cause of sleeping issues, first speak to your pediatrician. Constipation is more common with formula-fed babies and is often due to the type of formula they are being fed. Constipation can also occur when your baby is dehydrated and not getting enough fluid.

A baby who has diarrhea will poop more frequently and it will be much waterier and looser. Many babies will not fuss much when they have diarrhea. However, if not resolved quickly, this can quickly turn into dehydration which can cause a number of problems if not addressed immediately.

If you know your baby is suffering from some form of digestive issue, try feeding smaller amounts more frequently so that the stomach can properly handle what is being consumed. You might need to consider adjusting your diet if you breastfeed or changing formula if stomach issues are persistent. For instance, breastfed babies can suffer from stomach issues depending on what mom is eating. If you are consuming too much chocolate, dairy, or caffeine, this can upset your baby's tummy, too.

Try to eliminate these common culprits from your diet one at a time waiting a week between each elimination to see if this helps ease your baby's upset stomach. If you are formula feeding, speak to your pediatrician about switching to a lactose-free or soy-based formula. Many digestive issues in newborns are quickly corrected when their diet is modified slightly.

- ***Teething***

Though your little one may not show their first teeth until around the six-month mark, they can begin to teeth as early as two months. This is a painful process for your baby. Teething is often overlooked as the cause for many baby sleep problems.

Some of the most common signs that your baby is teething is an increase in saliva. Your baby is going to drool an impressive amount when they have teeth about to come in. This can make sleep uncomfortable because they can be more fussy or sensitive to any wetness they feel from their sheets or blankets. They can also develop a slight rash or skin irritation on their face, neck, or chest from being constantly wet.

Fevers are not always common in teething babies but a slight rise in body temperature can occur. This increase in body temperature will almost never exceed 100.4 degrees Fahrenheit. If it does, contact your pediatrician immediately.

Massaging your baby's gums can help alleviate teething pain. Give your baby a frozen washcloth or something cool to chew on to help numb the area and reduce the swelling that can cause pain. Teething rings or toys can be especially useful though you need to avoid any products that contain gels in them; these can be easily damaged and the gel accidentally ingested by your little one.

- ***Immunization***

During the first year of your baby's life, they will need to have a number of immunizations. These will often cause your baby some mild discomfort and can be a stressful ordeal for some babies.

Immunization comes with a number of side-effects from slight fevers to vomiting and fussiness. The time of day your baby receives their immunization can impact their sleep. Studies have shown that babies who received their routine immunization after 1:30 pm slept better than those who received them earlier in the day (Franck, L 2011). If you know your baby is due for some of their shots, try to schedule their visit in the later afternoon so they will sleep better.

Body Temperature Factors that Affect Sleep

Body temperature fluctuates throughout the day and can cause children and babies to wake earlier than expected or have more trouble getting to sleep. When body temperature is high, which is common in the evening, it can cause children to be more energized or uncomfortable. This makes falling to sleep hard. In the early morning, body temperature drops significantly and can cause babies to wake up because they are too cold. Keeping these two factors in mind when putting the baby to sleep can help you dress your baby appropriately and adjust the room temperature to ensure your baby is comfortable all night long. Your baby's body temperature is affected directly by the temperature in the room they sleep in but humidity levels and air quality in the room can also pose problems when it comes to getting your baby to sleep through the night.

- ***Too Hot or Cold***

If your baby's room is too hot or too cold, this will affect their quality and quantity of sleep in a number of ways. When the room is too hot, it can be more of a struggle for your baby to regulate their core body temperature; this can make it difficult for them to breathe.

When the core body temperature is slightly lower than normal, this actually increases the production of melatonin in the body which can help keep your baby asleep. Again, ideally, you want your baby's room to be somewhere between 65 to 72 degrees Fahrenheit.

If you think the room is too hot or too cold, or you're having a hard time regulating the temperature, you can dress your baby appropriately to compensate. Dress your baby in layers and place them in a warmer sleeping sack if they appear to be too cold. Your baby's hands or feet may turn a bluish color when their core body temperature drops. While this can be alarming, the blueish color will often disappear once they have been warmed for a bit. If your baby is sweating or looks red and flushed, this is a clear sign that they are too hot and you can remove layers and place them in a more lightweight sleeping slack.

- ***Humidity***

When the humidity in your baby's sleeping room is too low, this can dry out their nasal passages and cause your baby to feel stuffy which will wake them from their sleep. During the winter months, it is common for the air in the home to be drier because of central or room heating. On the other hand, when humidity levels get too high, it can cause mold to grow and more allergens to be released into the air, which can also cause respiratory issues in your baby. The right humidity levels will keep your baby comfortable and can help loosen up mucus when your baby is congested.

Most indoor thermometers can keep track of humidity levels as well. You'll want to keep humidity levels around 50%. Keeping a humidifier in the baby's room can help maintain optimal humidity levels. Humidifiers need to be cleaned properly and regularly so they do not spread bacteria. When cleaning a humidifier, you need to avoid using any harsh chemicals that you would typically use to kill germs around your home. These can be released into the air your baby breathes. You should aim to clean the humidifier at least every three days. Change the water in the humidifier daily.

- *Fresh Air or Lack of It*

Stagnant air can be difficult to continuously breathe. If your baby is in a room where the airflow is poor and there isn't a constant source to let in fresh air, this may cause or contribute to sleep disturbances.

To help keep the air circulating in your baby's sleeping room, turn on a ceiling fan or keep a small indoor fan running on low. This also provides your baby with a soft bit of noise which can be comforting and help ease them to sleep. Just be sure that portable fans are not aimed directly in the baby's sleeping direction.

External Factors that Affect Sleep

External factors are the most common things that affect baby sleep, and the easiest to correct. These are primarily in the sleeping environment. Making adjustments to any of the following elements can improve sleep significantly.

- ***Noise***

Many parents think that a quiet environment is the best environment for a baby to sleep. However, this is often not the case. Babies sleep better when there is a little bit of noise going on. They learn to sleep through distraction when regular noise is maintained during their daytime naps. Trying to keep a completely quiet home while your baby sleeps is incredibly appealing. You want your little one to sleep but this can hinder their ability to fall asleep on their own as they get older.

White noise has been shown to help promote better sleep for babies and adults alike. This is true even for babies who don't seem to need the noise to stay asleep. When your baby reaches a certain age, they are more interested in what is going on around them. This means that even the slightest noise in the middle of the night can cause them to wake up. White noise "disguises" these types of sounds. White noise is also helpful when you are transitioning from one of their comfort sleep time cues, such as swaddling.

Using a white noise machine can help your baby associate a calming and comforting noise with sleep. This can be especially useful to your little one as they grow. They will learn to sleep through such distractions like light, teething, minor illnesses, and even the noise of a television. The key to the effectiveness of a noise machine is to only have it running during the evening bedtime. You don't want your child to be exposed to the white noise all day since this will have the opposite effect on their sleep. It will also hinder their development because they wouldn't be exposed to new or different noises during the day.

Some of the best white noises to incorporate into your baby's bedtime routine are those of natural sounds, such as rain or waves crashing. Keep the volume of the noise machine low as your baby sleeps. Many parents find their baby is able to fall asleep faster when the machine is at a slightly higher volume and then decreasing the volume once the baby has fallen asleep. Some parents have successfully used quiet classical music as 'white noise.' Experiment to see what works best for you and your baby.

- ***Movement***

Babies will be easily distracted by what is going on around them. If there is too much movement happening around them, it will be hard for them to settle into sleep and stay asleep. For example, make sure that, when your baby is sleeping, there aren't people constantly running back and forth in front of the door; this can cause the lighting to change and awaken them. You also want to avoid going in and out of the room where they are sleeping. This can suddenly wake your baby or cause them to remain awake when they haven't yet fallen asleep.

- ***Lighting***

Newborns have yet to learn the difference between day and night and one way to help them identify this difference is to expose them to as much natural light during the day as possible. When it comes to teaching your baby to fall asleep on their own, light can help encourage nighttime sleep. If your baby is constantly put to sleep in a room that is too bright, they can struggle to identify when it is actually night. This can throw off their natural sleep cycle or circadian rhythm. If the room is too dark, your baby may feel uneasy, especially as they grow older, and their imagination can get the best of them.

You can help encourage healthy sleep habits by closing the blinds during daytime naps in your baby's room. You might also consider blackout blinds/curtains to darken the room. For the evening, you'll want to dim the lights before you start your bedtime routine so they can begin to associate the lower lights with sleep. Try to use warm lights in your baby's room when it is nighttime (red or yellow) as these will help maintain the production of melatonin.

Some parents put a night light in their baby's room to help them sleep but this can actually stop the production of melatonin. It is best to try to keep the baby's room as dark as possible. Doing this from the very beginning when you bring your baby home will get them accustomed to sleeping in the dark as they grow. This can reduce the likelihood that they will go through an "I'm scared of the dark" phase, since they will already be used to their room not having any lights. For nighttime feedings and changes, use a dim warm light and try to only turn it on if absolutely necessary.

Additional lighting factors to address are blue lights. Blue light is given off by many electronic devices from televisions to phones and tablets. This light has been shown to reduce the production of melatonin. LED lights and fluorescent bulbs run on this same shorter wavelength. Being exposed to blue light actually signals the body that it is not the time for sleep. With excessive exposure to blue light, even if you may be feeling tired, your body won't produce melatonin to help initiate sleep. The same applies to your baby.

Best Sleep Environment

1. Use a white noise machine.
2. Keep room dark and only use warm lighting.
3. No blue light.
4. Room temperature 65-72 degrees F.
5. Humidity around 50%
6. Limit movement from others inside the room.
7. Keep air circulating.
8. Schedule shots after 1:30pm

CHAPTER 7:

BABY SLEEP: STEP-BY-STEP AND AGE-BY-AGE COACHING FOR SLEEPING SCHEDULES

I feel like we are going backwards. Just a few months ago Olivia was sleeping almost through the night. She is 8 months old now, so we know that at least one middle of the night feeding is necessary. But we have now gone from one nighttime feeding to three or more! At least one of these times she is up for over an hour. I thought we had a handle on her sleep schedule and had a consistent routine established. Now, I feel we have just wasted so much time and energy getting her to sleep on only to revert back to old habits to get her to fall asleep quicker. Any ideas? -Lindsey.

Your baby's sleeping habits depend on, and change, according to their age. So, it's important for parents to know about the peculiarities of every age. When you don't understand what is changing in your little ones, you will be more likely to fall back into unhealthy sleep habits with your child.

There are recommendations for the average amount of sleep a baby should get. However, these are not the norm for every child. Some children need a little extra sleep and others are happy and healthier with a little less sleep. The recommended hours of sleep serve as a starting point for how much your baby should be sleeping according to their age. Keep in mind that each child develops differently and has different temperaments that will impact their sleep. Just because it is recommended that your baby get a certain number of hours of day-time or night sleep, that does not mean this is a strict guideline to follow.

Five Age Stages When Sleeping Habits are Formed and Changed

Sleep regression will occur periodically over the course of your little one's life. In the first few months, their sleeping habits will change a great deal until they settle into daytime and nighttime routines. Sleep regressions are typical and can often leave parents wondering what happened to their perfect little sleeper. Remember, these brief periods are only temporary and consistency with your bedtime routine and care is vital for quickly getting back to the desired sleep schedule.

Your baby will go through five distinct stages in the first few years and each stage has a number of factors that can interrupt healthy sleep. Understanding the way your baby is developing and changing during these times will help alleviate stress from sudden sleep changes. This will help you quickly make adjustments to their sleep routine to coincide with their developmental stage.

Three to Five Months

This time period is the most ideal to begin teaching your baby long-term healthy sleep habits. They have just come out of the newborn phase and are more active and interested in what is happening around them. At the three-month milestone, your baby is becoming more alert and responding more to external factors. They are becoming more engaged in social interactions and can be easily distracted by all the new things in their environment. Your baby will become more interested in toys and will begin to make verbal connections.

When they hit the four-month mark, the sleep cycle begins to significantly change. The length of the sleep they need decreases, their sleep cycle changes, and how deeply they're sleeping begins to adjust to their new sleep cycle. How much time they spend in NREM sleep and REM sleep makes a huge shift. Children around this age will sleep for longer stretches of time though most only sleep for about four to six hours at a time. Their total sleep averages around 17 hours which includes night-time sleep and nap time.

Sleep regression is likely during these months as your baby is trying to adapt to all the changes their body is going through including changes to their sleep cycle. Some babies easily fall into a natural routine with the sleep cycle. Many, however, are unsettled by these rapid changes. They may start falling into a deep NREM sleep which can be hard for the baby to adjust to. Your child is beginning to develop their own sleep-wake cycles during this stage.

At this time, your baby is more distractible as well. They are learning how to move their bodies and interact with their surroundings and this is a far more appealing activity than sleeping. A number of babies will want to take the time they have in their cribs to practice the new skills they are learning like rolling over, placing their hands to their mouth, kicking their legs, or simply watching what is going on in the room. Since your baby doesn't need as much sleep, they will want to spend more time interacting with others.

Babies at this age need a good amount of interaction and daily stimulation. There is a fine-line, however, of babies becoming overstimulated which can result in excess fatigue. Understanding and recognizing your baby's sleep cues is important during this time. In the evening, it is still typical that babies will wake every three to four hours to be fed.

Sleep training tips:

This is the ideal time to start incorporating healthy sleep associations and routines. Attempting to stick to a rigid sleep schedule will interfere with the child's ability to develop their natural sleep cycle. Keeping track of your baby's sleeping and waking hours can help you best formulate an appropriate sleep plan.

During awake hours, you'll want to expose your

child to as much natural sunlight as possible. This helps them begin to identify between day and night. When it gets closer to the evening bedtime, slowly reduce their exposure to natural sunlight. Using dim light as you go through your bedtime routine will help their body prepare for sleep.

Make the routine easy and predictable by utilizing the three B's:

- Bath
- Book
- Bed

You can incorporate smaller activities into the three B's, such as a soft massage after bath time, and, of course, feeding right before bed and turning on a white noise machine.

One of the first sleeping props you'll begin eliminating will be the swaddle. Your baby is beginning to move about more and breaking free anyways. Swaddling can be replaced with rocking or holding your baby to sleep. They get used to falling asleep on their own by placing them in their crib just as they are about to drift off.

Six to Eight Months

At this age, your baby is becoming more physically active and may start suffering through their teething phase. At six to eight months, a baby should be learning to sit with support and to roll themselves from a back-lying position to a front-lying position. A month after they accomplish this, they should be able to roll from front to back position. Your baby is also beginning to babble and react to the sound of your voice. They will smile and coo when they hear you and will mimic your facial expressions.

This is also the time when most parents begin to introduce solids into their baby's feeding schedule. Although it will take some time before solid food becomes the predominant food, this can still be a new and unsettling experience for babies. It can cause digestive issues as bowel movements may become more solid.

Babies at this age are prone to wake more frequently during the night than they have in the previous months. This is due to the rapid increase in cognitive development as well as changes in diet and movement/activity overall.

Once your baby reaches the six to eight-month mark, they will often settle into a more organized sleep pattern. They can sleep for longer periods of time through the night without waking but most babies will still wake a few times in the night. Naps are more consistent and predictable but may begin to affect nighttime sleep more. Many babies will fall into having a morning, mid-morning, and mid-afternoon nap. These naps are often an hour or two in length averaging about three and a half hours in total. Most of the sleep they get should occur in the nighttime hours which can stretch on for about 11 hours. Night feedings do still occur at this age, with only a small percentage of babies sleeping through the night.

The length of time babies in this age group spend in REM sleep decreases from 50% to 30% of the total sleep time. At this age, the biggest struggle parents tend to have is finding the right balance for keeping their baby awake and active long enough to encourage easy sleep. At the same time, you want to avoid accidentally keeping your baby awake for too long, which causes excess tiredness. Typically, babies at this age can spend about two hours awake before needing sleep.

Sleep training tips:

Most babies will fall asleep naturally, between 6:30 and 8:00 pm, for their long night sleep. It is not uncommon for parents to suddenly find themselves having to wake up more often throughout the night to feed their baby. It's easy to slip back into old habits of feeding your little one back to sleep. Unfortunately, they receive comfort from this familiar habit and the whole weaning process may have to be reimplemented.

To stick to a better sleep routine, it is important to set nap times and keep a consistent bedtime. Keeping in mind that your baby will often be awake for two hours in between naps, you can easily come up with a schedule that fits your family's needs. For example, if you want your little one to be in bed by 7 pm every night and ideally sleep for 11 to 12 hours through the night, their wake-up time should be around 7 am. Their first nap should take place around 9 am, their third nap should fall around 12:30 and their fourth nap will be around 4 pm and will often be shorter. Then you can begin your bedtime routine by 6:30 pm and have them into bed by 7 pm.

During these bedtime routines, you want to incorporate nighttime phrases to reinforce that it's time for bed. If your baby begins to cry when you leave them in their bed, you'll want to begin to wean them from needing your presence in the room. Often, this begins with you holding them for a few minutes until they are calm and relaxed, and then placing them back in the crib. Then you comfort them by holding your hand on their stomach and humming to them. Finally, you should be able to leave the room while your little one is drifting off to sleep. If they do wake up shortly after you leave, comfort them again by placing a hand on their stomach and humming to them.

At this age, they begin getting used to sleeping through the night. For many, this means that nighttime feedings will become less frequent. It is also a good time to incorporate sleep training techniques, such as placing your baby in their crib when they are drowsy but not fully asleep yet, to help them fall asleep on their own.

Nine to Twelve Months

During this time, your baby is really starting to move. They will most likely begin crawling or sliding along the floors. Remember that the lumbar spine develops its forward curve when the baby begins crawling so allow them this opportunity. Many babies learn to pull themselves up to a standing position and are able to pick up and drop or throw toys. They have now learned their own name and begin to associate the fact that, even though he or she may not see an object or person, they are still there. Practicing new skills can also hinder a baby's sleep routine since they want to practice whenever they can. This often results in them trying to pull themselves up in their crib or crawl from one side of their crib to the other.

Common concerns at this age occur when a baby is not sitting up on their own or if they are not able to support their own weight when standing. Other concerns can arise if the baby is not able to move objects from one hand to another or if there are issues with introducing solids such as refusing food, gagging, or spitting up after eating solids. Talk to your pediatrician about any developmental concerns you may have.

During this time, separation anxiety can and often does occur. This can cause nighttime sleeping to become a major issue, especially because many parents begin to transition the baby into their own bedrooms. Even if your baby has been sleeping soundly for the last few months, at this age, many are likely to feel stressed when their parents are not in the same room.

Afternoons can be a stressful time for parents and babies as the midday nap is dropped leaving only two nap-times. This can be addressed by moving up their later nap and trying to get the baby to go to bed earlier in the evening. Naps will typically last for one to two hours but their night sleep amount usually remains the same.

Sleep training tips:

If you are moving your baby into their own room for sleep, it is best to begin doing this with their naps first. This allows them to become more comfortable in their new surroundings.

When sleep issues occur in the evening, it's often due to their nap schedule. Dropping down to two naps at this time, can often improve benign sleep. At this age, babies stay awake for longer stretches before they need a nap, and often will give you clear cues when this is necessary.

Most babies will not need middle-of-the-night feedings at this stage, and their waking in the middle of the night to be fed is more likely out of habit instead of hunger. Many parents tend to continue with night feedings without understanding that it is completely normal for young children at this age to wake up for a brief time and then fall back to sleep. If you notice this still occurring, you will want to give your baby the opportunity to soothe themselves back to sleep before rushing in to assist them or feed them.

When your baby wakes in the morning, avoid feeding them right away. You want to give them about ten to fifteen minutes of being awake before their first feeding. This reduces them associating waking in the morning with feeding. It will allow them to establish this time as the start of their day and not just a time to be fed on demand. This delay can be accomplished by substituting another activity, such as changing them and chatting with them while you are preparing their first meal.

If you haven't started already, this is the time to begin weaning the baby off any additional sleeping props, like a pacifier, to teach them to sleep independently.

One and a Half Years to Two and a Half Years

This is a blissful age where your little one's personality begins to shine. With this bliss, however, comes a bit more combativeness at bedtime.

Once asleep, they are more likely to sleep through the night. Sleep is less broken than it has been in the previous months. At the one-year mark, your baby usually begins walking or, at least, cruising along the furniture. Babies at this age can understand and follow simple directions like "come here." They recognize familiar faces and songs. They also love the attention they get from family members. Most children around this age eat a wide range of solids and will often take part in family mealtimes instead of being bottle-fed.

Sleep is impaired by a number of factors at this age. Your baby is becoming quite mobile and their ability to move around on their own causes them to be both more energized and excited throughout the day. This means that they are also prone to become overly-tired. Learning to speak, being introduced to new foods, forming teeth, and other developmental changes also make sleep less appealing for babies at this age.

It is not uncommon for parents to have to revise the basic needs of their babies to aid in better sleep. Is your baby getting the proper foods and amounts of food throughout the day? Is your child giving you the right cues when they are becoming sleepy and need to lay down for a nap? Are they getting enough movement during the day and enough natural sunlight? Are you giving your baby enough love and encouragement throughout the day so they are not seeking more of it in the evening?

It is also vital that they are given the opportunity to explore their new ability to move around and use their words to ask for what they need. They can become frustrated with the process and require a bit of parental reassurance and support in learning to improve their new skills.

Naps are often limited to two times per day. An evening snack can help keep them satisfied throughout and prevent middle-of-the-night waking. Around the 15 to 16-month mark, your baby may begin to drop down to just one nap a day. Their evening sleep often lasts for about 10 to 12 hours and naps are often two hours long.

Just before their two-year birthday, your little one is exploring their surroundings in new ways, by climbing, jumping or running from room to room. They are interested in more functional play like turning the pages of a book, moving cars along the floor, stacking blocks, and organizing shapes and colors. Your child is becoming more independent and may be able to play for short periods of time on their own. They are more interested in singing and dancing which helps them strengthen the skills they need to balance and communicate.

Some red flags at this age can include:

- Your child is not walking
- Poor hand control
- Balance issues
- Stiff or rigid body movement
- Feeding problems

Do not hesitate to consult with a professional with any of these concerns. Your child is more mobile at this age, and it is not uncommon for them to struggle with sleep. This can be a frustrating time for your little one, as they are understanding more of what is being said to them but are not able to communicate well to their parents about their needs or wants. Tantrums can become more frequent as they become easily frustrated in the inability to effectively communicate or feel understood and heard by their parents.

Separation anxiety can also occur at this age, as your child is eager for more independence but still needs comfort and reassurance from you. Many children can become clingy at this age and it can mean having a great deal of patience, consistency, gentle boundaries, and compassion. Incorporating limited choices throughout the day can help your child feel more confident and can fulfill their need for independence.

Your baby may begin to bring their newfound climbing skills into the bed with them and escape in the middle of the night or, more likely, right after being put to bed. Around this time, many parents begin to transition their children to a toddler bed which can create sleep troubles because the child needs to get used to their new sleeping arrangements.

The increase in brain activity that occurs during this time frame can cause children to wake up in the middle of the night. Because of how much their brain is working during the day and how much they have to process at night, sleep is often neglected.

Most children around the age of two do not wake up in the middle of the night to feed. It's more common for them to wake up from night terrors, nightmares, or bed wetting.

Sleep training tips:

1. At this age, your child may need to have their evening bedtime adjusted. If they are waking up earlier than expected they can benefit from a slightly later bedtime.

2. Being consistent with your sleep training efforts is crucial during this age because many children have already formed sleeping habits that often need to be replaced with more independent techniques.
3. Eliminate screen time at least one hour prior to bed to reduce exposure to blue light.
4. If potty training, avoid giving liquids at least one hour before bed.

At this age, your child may be calling for you in the middle of the night because they *want* you with them and not because they necessarily *need* you. You want to comfort your child and reassure them that they are safe, but this can lead to an increase in nighttime wake-ups. In this situation, implementing fading techniques can help your child feel more secure when they are falling asleep and can also ease them back to sleep when they wake in the middle of the night and don't see you there.

Three Years to Five Years

At this age, children are spending about 25% of their time in REM sleep. They sleep for approximately 13 hours and will have dropped their daytime nap. Many children may still need an occasional nap here and there. Some may continue with a short midday nap every day, but will generally be reluctant and resist napping.

When a child resists a nap, it can be a clear indication they may no longer need it. It is best to look for behaviors and emotional cues that will allow you to make the best choice in terms of cutting or keeping the daytime nap. If your child has no issue with taking a nap during the day and it doesn't affect their ability to get to sleep in the evening, then there is no reason to cut the nap.

If, however, your child is fighting you on taking a nap, and the naps are quite short, it may be time to eliminate them. If your child is still taking an afternoon nap but they are struggling to get to bed at an appropriate hour, you might want to begin cutting out the nap. If your child is not overly tired during the day, is appropriately managing their emotions, and is not going to bed too early (which then results in early waking time), then an afternoon nap is most likely not necessary.

For the most part, parents often choose to drop naps entirely when persistent issues arise that are interfering with the nighttime routine. Until then, many parents allow their toddlers to take a midday nap when they need it and skip it when they are happy and well-rested without it.

This is the age where most potty training begins to take place. There is a greater chance that your child will wake in the middle of the night needing to be changed into clean clothes. Many children at this age are either starting to attend daycare or will begin pre-school. Some families may be expanding and your toddler may be getting a new sibling.

Children at this age are expanding on their motor

skills, learning to run, or even beginning to ride a bike. They are more independent and are eager to gain more independence. They begin to form new relationships with classmates and teachers. At this age, sleep can be disrupted due to all the new connections they are making with others. This is also the age when developmental issues, due to lack of sleep, become more obvious.

Sleep Training Ideas

If your child is still struggling to fall asleep independently, and there is no medical condition that can account for these issues, it may be time to take a more formal approach to their bedtime routine. You may need to set boundaries for sleep, for example, helping them to understand that bedtime is not meant for playing. This means no loud or big toys, no television, no running around, and no calling you back into the bedroom for a hundred different reasons.

Establishing clear bedtime rules allows your child

to create a bedtime routine that will help them fall asleep on their own. Make it clear that you will not be coming back in to check on them every five minutes because they lost their stuffed animal or their blankets are not covering them fully.

Sleep By Age

Age	Total Sleep	Number of Naps	Nap Length	Evening Sleep
3 to 5 months	17 hrs	4 or more	1-2 hrs	6-8 hrs
6 to 8 months	15 hrs	3	1-2 hrs	8-11 hrs
9 to 12 months	15 hrs	2-3	1-2 hrs	8-11 hrs
1-1/2 to 2-1/2 years	14 hrs	2	2 hrs	10-12 hrs
3 to 5 years	13 hrs	1-0	2 hrs	10-12 hrs

How to Avoid Common Mistakes

It is never too late to teach good sleeping habits. But it must be understood that there are typically no quick fixes. There is no set time frame for when parents can expect to see improvement or changes in their child's sleep patterns. This can often be discouraging to parents who are desperate to find a solution for their own sleep deprivation but it takes patience and consistency. Avoid these common mistakes when you decide that it is time to sleep coach your baby.

1. Many parents will jump into one method of sleep coaching, even if they are not 100% invested in the steps needed to implement the strategy. When this occurs, they may not give the technique enough time before jumping into another routine.
2. It takes a few weeks for adults to form a new habit, and even then, it's only successful when consistently implemented. Babies take much longer to develop new habits. As a general rule, you may see some progress in your child's sleeping within a few days or weeks, but most likely, their default pattern will persist for many weeks. Gentle sleeping approaches can make the transition feel less stressful despite the lack of sleep one may be

getting. Providing your baby with comfort and soothing techniques, that will teach them to fall asleep on their own, is the goal of a gentle approach. You and your baby will be in better spirits around bedtime.

3. It is especially frustrating when you begin to make significant progress only to face a development change in your baby. Teething, illness, and growth can cause children to be thrown off from their typical sleeping patterns. This can make it feel as if all the progress made was pointless and a waste of time. Do not lose faith, these are temporary setbacks. You can get back on track if you continue with the basics. Sticking with a bedtime routine, whether it results in the baby falling asleep or not, is essential. This reinforces these routines with sleep time. Even after your child has gone through the teething and growing phase, they will have

formed these strong connections with the activities that come just before bedtime.

4. Most parents have a general understanding that if they wait to put their baby to sleep, wake them up earlier from naps, or drop naps altogether, their baby will sleep longer in the evening. When we are tired, we tend to sleep longer and can quickly fall asleep in the evening. Becoming overtired, however, can cause problems with getting your baby to sleep. Unlike adults, babies have not developed the proper skills or tools to manage the behaviors, emotions, and the mental fatigue that comes from being overly tired.
5. Adults combat their feelings of being overtired by producing the hormones, cortisol, and adrenaline. For adults, these hormones help give a boost of energy. However, in a child, these hormones can trigger other physiological changes that keep them aroused when they should be

sleeping. Parents often think that when their baby falls asleep rather quickly, they are developing healthy sleep habits. In fact, they may actually be severely sleep-deprived. When the baby is overtired, they are going to feel more discomfort and stress. Children need to shift from awake to sleep in a slow and gradual way. Jumping straight into sleep can cause them to jump into the rest of their cycle too quickly which can result in a shorter sleep time.

6. Allow your baby to sleep with their socks on. The feet play a major role in regulating body temperature and in the early hours, they will need extra warmth to keep them from waking up too early because they are cold.
7. Have a set, yet flexible bedtime. You don't need to stick to a strict schedule that is enforced to the minute, but you do need to agree upon a desirable time frame to aim

for. Realistically, if you come within 30 minutes either before or after that desired time, consider it an accomplishment. You need to allow for this grace period to reduce stress and maintain a calm state of mind through the sleep coaching process.

8. Establish a predictable bedtime routine. This is one of the most important factors needed to develop healthy sleeping habits. A predictable routine is one that should be the go-to throughout their early years and into their young school-aged years. If the bedtime routine is not consistent, you can expect your little one to have inconsistency in their sleeping behaviors.
9. Cut out screen time before bed. This is common knowledge but is often the one thing that parents are reluctant to enforce when it comes to creating a successful bedtime routine. It is very likely that everyone will gather around the TV as a calm-down time

right before bed, and while it may appear to be keeping the kids quiet and occupied, it is actually overstimulating their brain. Screen time should be cut out at least two hours prior to the desired bedtime; electronics like TV, smartphones, and tablets should be kept out of the bedroom.

10. Avoid using the bedroom as a punishment. This is a common mistake that parents unknowingly make. The bedroom should be a place for calmness and security. If you send your child to their room as a punishment, this can unintentionally teach them to have a negative view of their bedroom. This can also result in anxiety. The opposite can occur as well. If a child is constantly in their bedroom jumping around, being loud, and exerting a great deal of energy during the time they spend in their room, it can be challenging for them to switch into a calmer mode when it is time to sleep.

CHAPTER 8:

TROUBLESHOOTING SLEEP ISSUES

The nightmares began when Veronica was about 3 years old. All of a sudden, she was waking multiple nights during the week. Despite us checking under the bed, in the closet, and outside her window, nothing makes her feel safe enough to stay asleep. We don't allow her to watch anything scary, but it seems her imagination is getting the best of her. We've added nightlights to her room, keep the door cracked open, and she even has stuffed animals that light to help her fall back asleep when she is frightened. Nothing seems to be helping. How can we teach her that there is nothing to be afraid of so we can all get back to our normal bedtime routine? - Erykah and Charles.

Most parents will, at some point, have to deal with an "imaginary" sleep disturbance. Sleeping issues and disorders often depend on the sleep environment which can inadvertently cause heavy sleep problems, psychological issues, instability, physical disorders, and more. Parents should be aware of these problems while making changes in life routines.

Let's see if we can help Veronica with her night scares.

Nightmares, Night Terrors, Sleeping Walking, and Other Sleep Interruptions

A majority of children, even if they have had no sleep problems in the past, can suddenly have parasomnias. These are specific sleep disorders that cause a child to have abnormal movements in sleep and can also cause behavioral, emotional, and skewed perceptions of dreams. While these conditions can be a scary experience for parents and children, they are often not an indication of psychological or emotional disorder in children, and are, generally, nothing to worry about.

The most common parasomnias include nightmares, night terrors, and sleepwalking but can also include:

- Confusional arousal (acting strangely when first waking up)
- Sleep talking
- Teeth grinding
- Rhythmic-movement disorder (unusual muscle movements prior to falling asleep)
- Nocturnal enuresis (bed wetting)

These conditions can occur at different ages and, over time, tend to disappear on their own. Understanding what the most common conditions are, how they appear, and when to expect them to occur can give you a head start in having strategies in place to handle them and ease your child back to sleep. If you have any concerns, contact your pediatrician.

Nightmares

Nightmares can occur at any age but become more distinguishable when a child is over the age of two. A child may or may not awake fully from a nightmare as they take place when the child is in REM sleep. Nightmares cause children to have terrifying and highly vivid dreams which often triggers the stress response system in the body. Though children of any age can experience these sleep disturbances, they are more likely to appear when a child is dealing with stress in their lives, or a big change in routine or structures is taking place.

Dealing with nightmares can be as simple as placing a nightlight in the child's room and providing them with a lot of reassurance that they are safe and you are right there with them. Try not to feed into the idea of scary monsters under the bed or ghosts in the closet which are common precursors to a child having a nightmare. Checking under the bed or in the closest reinforces the idea that something scary may be lurking in the dark. You want to take a more logical approach by hearing their fear but also reassuring them that most of their fears are just in their imagination or unrealistic.

Night Terrors

Night terrors can be a terrifying experience for parents, too. These occur in the NREM sleep cycle and are more common in children from the age of three to five. Night terrors can give the appearance that your child is fully awake and having a fit. For instance, they will often scream and cry inconsolably. Many will thrash about in their beds, hit, and be completely out of control.

My second son suffered from night terrors at a young age. When they first began, I would rush into his room and try to hug and comfort him. I thought he was awake and just scared from a nightmare. But every time I came close to him, he would panic even more and begin to hit and kick at me. The more I tried to reassure him that I was there, the more enraged he seemed to become. His eyes were open but at the time I was clueless that he was still in mid-sleep.

When night terrors occur, they can immediately alarm parents, especially since children have no recollections of them upon waking in the morning. They can be incredibly intense and terrifying to witness. The best thing to do when they occur is to ensure that your child is safe in their own bed. My son was sleeping in a toddler bed at the time when he started to have night terrors. He would get out of bed and throw things around the room. We had to make adjustments to his sleep environment so that he wouldn't harm himself or anyone else when they suddenly happened again. While our experience with night terrors was more of an extreme case, many children have much milder experiences.

Most often, night terrors are common when a child is overtired. They occur more frequently in children who tend to be potty training and sometimes happen in the middle of the night just before a child is about to urinate. Modifying the sleep routine may be necessary to ensure the child is getting to bed at a more decent hour. If you have yet to start a bedtime routine, night terrors are a good indication that it might be a good idea to do so.

Sleepwalking

Sleepwalking is not uncommon, and is more typical in younger children as opposed to adults. Sleepwalking takes place in the child's NREM sleep cycle, as well. They'll sit up, walk around, and sometimes talk and have conversations. Some children even keep their eyes open as they are sleepwalking making it a challenge for parents to know when it is happening at first.

Sleepwalking is often the result of a child being overly tired. When sleepwalking occurs, the child can and should be wakened gently and guided back to their bed. If you are concerned about your child falling or hurting themselves when they sleep walk, a gate may be necessary to put in the child's doorway or to block off access to stairs. Special child-proof door knobs or out-of-reach locks on doors to the outside, basements, or other areas of the home can also be utilized to better ensure their safety, if they are going through a period of sleepwalking.

Sensory Processing Disorder, Spectrum Disorder, and ADHD

Anthony was never a good sleeper. From the day we brought him home, sleep just didn't come easy. We had hoped he would grow out of it and provided him with extra snuggles and love. As he got older, the issues seemed to get worse. He wasn't a happy baby. When he began to walk and move around more, it was like he was running on a motor. He was just always on the go. With the little sleep he was getting, I was clueless as to how he had so much energy during the day. Maybe he just doesn't need as much sleep as other children? Upon your recommendation we spoke to his pediatrician about our concerns. It has been mentioned that we do further evaluation for ASD. Hearing this is like facing our worst fears. We know the challenges we will face with an Autism diagnosis, but does this mean we are doomed to endure sleepless nights indefinitely? - Brooklyn and Devin.

Developmental and neurological disorders often contribute to significant sleep issues in young children. With the increase in diagnoses for Autism Spectrum Disorder, Attention Deficit Disorder, and Sensory Processing Disorder, it is very likely that parents will encounter the struggles that come with these issues. These conditions have major effects on daily behaviors and are worsened by sleep troubles. We will take a closer look at each condition, the symptoms, and how you can help your child if they've been diagnosed or are suspected of having one or more of these issues.

Sensory Processing Disorder

Sensory processing disorder can take on many forms and relate to one or all of the senses. These children can be easily overstimulated by sensory factors or can have a higher tolerance of sensory stimulation which causes them to seek out what they need. Either condition can cause children to exhibit inappropriate behaviors, have difficulty functioning, and can impair sleep.

Some children may need to spin, jump, or feel physical pressure in order to gather important information or feedback from their surroundings. Other children will need limited exposure to lights, sounds, and action. If a child seeks or avoids certain sensory stimulations, they can become easily stressed; this can be incredibly hard for a young child to express to parents or caregivers.

Sensory seekers who have a need for more movement or deep pressure tend to have a slower heart rate, which is why they seek out more stimulation so their body can regulate their heartbeat. Sensory aversion occurs in children who tend to have a faster heartbeat which can trigger the fear response in the body so that they want to avoid certain sensory situations.

While it is not entirely uncommon for children or adults to have sensory needs, this becomes a concern when they begin to interfere with daily routines. The stress that one can feel from not having these sensory needs fulfilled can severely impact their ability to sleep and function well when awake.

Some children may have a few sensory needs that are not an issue, others may have a variety of sensory needs that are manageable. What is important is that parents consider the sensory needs their child is seeking or avoiding, to help them better understand and make adjustments to routines to help cope with these issues. A fussy or whiny baby who doesn't sleep well may not be just a difficult baby. They may be in need of certain stimulation to help their body feel calm enough for sleep.

There are many ways to address sensory needs which can include giving your child extra time for movement during the day, deep pressure massage, blanket rolling, and vestibular activities (jumping, dancing, marching, etc.). Most children will have little ticks when it comes to sensory issues. Some children have issues with tags on clothing or the feel of the fabric on their skin. Understanding your child's specific sensory needs can take some time to uncover but there are plenty of ways to address these issues throughout the day so they aren't interfering with your child's sleep at night.

Children with sensory seeking tendencies tend to have a harder time falling asleep, since bedtime is often devoid of many sensory inputs. Children can become hyper-aroused because they are not receiving any type of sensory inputs or are not getting enough of certain inputs, like not having heavy enough blankets or their pajamas are too loose. Children who are more sensitive to external stimulation may find nightlights, noise machines, tight clothing or swaddles, to be overstimulating which can cause them to feel distressed when it is time to sleep.

Autism Spectrum Disorder (ASD)

Autism Spectrum Disorder (ASD) encompasses a broad range of characteristics. Children diagnosed with ASD have challenges with their social skills, communication, and behaviors. It is considered a developmental disability and symptoms can include:

- Lack of interest in other people
- Limited verbal skills
- Self-stimulating behavior (such as hand-flapping or spinning)
- High threshold for pain or under-reacting to pain

- Increase in gross-motor movements
- Lack of fine-motor skills
- Sensitivity to noise

ASD is usually diagnosed in children under the age of three. Oftentimes, symptoms seem to appear out of nowhere. Most children develop fine, up until they are around 18-months-old when they tend to stop gaining additional skills. There are early signs that can indicate a child is on the spectrum, such as:

- Not recognizing their name by their first birthday
- Not playing with toys in a make-believe fashion
- Minimal, if any, eye contact
- Lack of emotional understanding
- Delay in speech or verbal skills
- Use of repeated words or phrases
- Easily stressed over minor changes
- Flapping hands, rocking, or spinning in circles

- Overreacting or reacting unusually to sensory input

There are a number of concerns that parents raising a child with ASD need to address and, unfortunately, often sleep tends to be one of the last. Children on the spectrum often have irregular sleep and waking patterns. They typically sleep much less than is recommended for children of their age and they tend to be more sensitive to light and sound. This lack of sleep can significantly increase any behavioral or emotional issues.

Most older children with ASD struggle with sleep issues and are often placed on medications to help manage symptoms. This can include antihistamines, sedatives, antidepressants, multivitamins, and medications to help with the production of melatonin.

Because these children develop at different rates than other children, it can be more difficult for parents to decide when to start sleeping training or, because of a later diagnosis, may be fighting to get their child to stick to a sleeping schedule when they are developmentally not ready. For many, room sharing with their child is one of the few ways they can get their child to relax enough to fall asleep but this inevitably results in the child waking up and needing to be calmed back to sleep.

While ASD creates obstacles for your child, sleep doesn't have to be one of them. When you are sure that you have ruled out any other medical conditions, such as sleep apnea, you can begin to incorporate simple bedtime routines that will help ease your child to sleep. Encouraging your child to get extra exercise during the day can help, including activities that meet their sensory needs. When it is nearing bedtime, you want to expose them to very little stimulation. Deep pressure massage, warm baths, and other calming activities are ideal for those who are on the spectrum. Keep in mind that you will need to introduce each new element to the bedtime routine one at a time so they are not easily upset by drastic changes.

Attention Deficit Hyperactivity Disorder (ADHD/ADD)

Children who are diagnosed with ADHD may struggle with many areas of sleep. They spend more time in sleep latency, tend to wake more frequently throughout the night, and have shorter repetitive sleep cycles. This fragmented and poor sleep can increase their symptoms, such as impulsivity, hyperactivity, an inability to concentrate, and a number of other general behavioral concerns.

While medication is the most common form of treatment, ADHD medication can interfere with sleep. Most of these treatments are stimulants like methylphenidate (Ritalin), which are known to cause sleep problems. Many children with ADHD already have difficulty sleeping which contributes even more to their behavioral and emotional issues. More holistic approaches should be combined with any medication options to combat other symptoms. Dietary changes and an increase in exercise can help promote better sleep in children with ADHD. Therapy may also be highly beneficial to help children regulate their emotions and provide them with the tools to manage their symptoms on their own.

Breaking from Routines

There are certain times when you have to break from some of your standard sleep routines. Aside from medical conditions, sleep disturbances, and developmental milestones, other factors like vacationing, hospital stays, and a move can set back your sleep training progress. While this can throw off your expected time line for getting your little one to sleep independently, they do not have to completely derail all your efforts so far.

What to do When you Need to Travel

Traveling is a time where you can really enjoy spending more time with your little one. It is also a time when many parents are more relaxed about sleeping schedules and routines. While it is tempting to allow your little one to stay up longer or skip a nap or two, you'll need to stick with some type of familiarity. Deviating from your baby's sleeping schedule too much can also cause problems once your vacation is over. Additionally, when you become lax about your baby not taking naps, you are going to have a more cranky and unhappy baby for your trip. Sticking to your routine, as much as possible, will allow you all to enjoy your vacation more.

There are some ways you can better stick to your baby's sleep schedule when you know you have a trip coming up.

1. If you are going to stay in a hotel, book a suite. A suit will allow your baby to sleep in their own room during naps and limits the other family members interrupting their sleep.
2. Plan meals that do not always involve having to go out to eat. Do a little bit of

research or ask the hotel front desk for a number of take-out options. Eating out at a restaurant with a baby can be a hassle. Trying to do it for three meals a day is just setting yourself up for additional stress that you can easily avoid.

3. Stick with your baby's bedtime routine. Sometimes this means your little one will fall asleep in the stroller and other times it means you will be going through your simple bath, bottle, and book routine in the hotel or family house. You want to try to stick with the simple bedtime process but don't stress out about strictly sticking with it.
4. Be sure to still allow your baby plenty of playtime. Parents tend to forget that, when they are walking around sightseeing and exploring a new place, their baby is often left in the stroller for a majority of the time. You still want to get your baby out and move, if they are able, whenever possible.

When you make your best efforts to stick to a minimal sleep routine while you are on vacation, it will make transitioning back into your regular routine, once you return, much easier. While you don't have to be as strict, there still needs to be some predictability so your baby can quickly adjust to the nap and evening sleep schedule.

During an Extended Hospital Stay

I hope your child never needs to stay in a hospital for an extended period of time. In a hospital, your child is in a very unfamiliar place, and can be even more stressed with all the comings and goings of nurses or doctors, not to mention all the different sounds that fill their rooms. There is no easy way to stick to a routine when you are expected to stay in a hospital. More often than not, parents tend to forgo their sleep training methods to provide extra comfort, cuddles, and anything else their baby needs at this time.

What can help baby sleep better is having some

familiar items with them? A favorite blanket or toy can soothe your baby to sleep when they are sick or hurt. Once returning from the hospital, you will want to give your baby a few days to adjust to being home again before picking up on the sleep coaching method you were implementing beforehand.

Moving

Moving is an exciting and chaotic time, whether you have a baby or not. For your baby, this can cause sleep problems to quickly arise. When you are planning to move, do your best to maintain the same sleep schedule throughout the process. This can be more challenging at this time; there will be more noise and people moving about. Aside from all the extra commotion, your baby will need to get used to sleeping in a new environment all over again.

You might have to take a few steps back in your sleep training method to help your baby feel more relaxed and settled in their new home. Constantly keeping a calming bedtime routine through the transition can be especially helpful when you are moved into your new place. Since your baby has already formed a strong association with their bedtime routine, it won't take long for them to feel comfortable with the same routine in a new environment.

CHAPTER 9:

BABY SLEEP: HOW TO BE A HAPPY PARENT

I have lost myself to being a mom. I feel like I am not allowed to do anything more than be a good mom to Jasey. I knew that being a parent meant making certain sacrifices, but I didn't think it meant having to give up everything I used to enjoy doing. My day is scheduled around her eating, napping, and playing. I don't even want to admit to how many days I go without showering. This isn't what motherhood is supposed to be like, is it? I am afraid that I am becoming more unhappy. Though I don't know if this is just due to not getting enough sleep, or really if it's because of how much I am neglecting myself. When do I get to start doing the things that I used to love doing? When will I not feel guilty for doing them? Am I a bad mom because I want to have some kind of identity aside from "mom"? - Meredith.

My heart goes out to every parent that comes to me with a situation similar to Meredith's. I was there once, too - giving everything I had to raising my boys and having little, if any, time leftover for myself. I struggled with whether I would be looked down on when I returned to work. I struggled to justify why it was important for me to have a night off. I struggled, even, with giving myself permission to enjoy things that didn't always involve my boys. We all want what is best for our children, and are willing to make any sacrifice to ensure they are healthy and happy. We focus so much of our attention on our children that we often ignore or avoid the signs that we need to take better care of ourselves.

A good parent does not mean we put ourselves last

all the time. A good parent means that we are balancing our lives. We tap into our knowledge, experience, readiness to learn, patience, and conscientiousness. At the same time, we make sure that we are taking care of ourselves with enough sleep, good nutrition, quiet time, and in pursuit of things we like to do. Without this balance, parenting becomes a heavy burden.

There is an array of parenting styles that we all fall into; authoritarian, authoritative, and permissive styles are the most common, and parents tend to go back and forth among these different styles when raising their child. An aware parent addresses many aspects of parenting that can be overwhelming. The gentler parenting approach, which is supported throughout this book and is one that I adhere to when raising my own children, teaches children the importance of compassion, kindness, empathy, and aligns with the individual's own beliefs and values.

There is no one-size-fits-all strategy for parenting.

We do, however, need to avoid falling into the accidental parenting category. This occurs when caregivers are exhausted and desperate. They constantly bounce from one style to another, blurring boundaries and creating a sense of uncertainty for the child. When you become more in tune with your own parenting style and understand how to utilize this style in a more mindful and conscious way, you can create a more cohesive and supportive environment for your baby and yourself.

Through conscious parenting, we learn our own limits. We nurture an unconditional and respectful relationship with our children from the first day and build upon that relationship to strengthen the mutual trust that makes a happy healthy family work.

Although this is not a book on child behavior and discipline techniques, it can certainly come into play when we are having difficulties with sleep training. Staying conscious to what your parenting style is, and how you might need to adjust it to create healthy but loving boundaries, can be the key to success in solving your baby's sleeping issues.

Knowledge is Essential

When you take on a more conscious approach to parenting, it will require a readiness to learn new approaches and combine them with ancient wisdom. When we make our choices out of love and the overall well-being of our child, then there is no right or wrong way to raise your child. This needs to be applied to ourselves as well.

We need to take the time to understand ourselves to build the foundations for how we teach our children the most important life skills including healthy sleep habits. Recognizing troublesome behaviors and taking a moment to step back from the situation to identify the root causes puts us in the mindset to respond to our child's needs instead of reacting to them. When we do this, it's easier to see that most of the behaviors that we are seeing from our infant, toddler, or young child are normal. We can then feel less anxious about forcing our child to stick with a sleep routine that does not align with where they are developmentally or within their own biological clockwork.

First-time parents need extra support as they transition into their new role of parenthood. Becoming a parent is a joyous time but it also means there are a number of changes that you may not have fully considered. You will find yourself confronting self-doubt, fear, guilt, and depression. Unfortunately, while you may be loving your little one day and night, you might be struggling, like many new parents, to maintain an identity outside of your role of 'mom' or 'dad.'

When I first had David, our oldest son, I thought for sure that we had the ideal plan in place. I would be able to take time off from work for the first six months to be at home with David. My husband's parents and mine would alternate watching David when I returned to work. As the six-month mark got closer, I was struggling with being able to return to work and just pick up where I had left off. I also began to question whether I wanted to be one of those working moms that let someone else raise their kids.

It was a flawed mindset that, eventually, began to consume me. We struggled with getting David to sleep throughout this entire time. Sleep deprivation was beginning to take its toll on me and, like many other parents, the first thing that was being affected was my self-confidence. Every little thing became a burden. I was overly critical of everything I was doing. This criticism stemmed from me not taking care of myself, and subconsciously thinking that it meant I was doing a poor job of taking care of David. This was not completely untrue. By not looking after my own needs I was unable to fully attend to David's.

I was not only neglecting myself; I was ignoring the red flags of postpartum depression. But there was no way that I could be suffering from depression – I thought. I had years of experience and taught other mothers how to cope with the demands of being a new mom. I thought that I would be the exception. No matter how much I tried to brush off my feelings as just the "baby blues" and normal parental worries, the overwhelming hopelessness was taking its toll.

One in seven women will suffer from postpartum depression (Carberg, 2019). This number only reflects the reported cases of postpartum depression. Thousands of women suffer in silence with this condition, never receiving the help they need. This doesn't just affect mothers. First time dads are just as likely to develop symptoms of depression as well.

Postpartum depression can go undetected for weeks and even months. This is due to the fact that it is often brushed off as 'normal.' Making the necessary changes when you have a new baby can be a lot to take in all at once. First-time parents are told that what they are feeling is what every new parent feels. The mood swings, anxiety, and difficulty sleeping are all "part of being a parent." However, this doesn't mean these emotions should be ignored. When you begin to constantly question your own abilities, and the fear of not being a good enough parent consumes your thoughts, this can result in serious mental health issues. Yes, it is common for parents to go through a number of intense emotions as they are raising a child. When this begins to interfere with your daily activities and sense of well-being, it is time to reach out for help.

Having a child is a lot of work. It requires a significant amount of energy and patience. If we are not giving ourselves the care we personally need, then we will not be able to commit to fully caring for our children the way we desire. My mom had given me some great advice. "If you try to pour from an empty cup, everyone will go thirsty." I wasn't taking the time to refill my depleted energy. I wasn't taking the time to do the things that I enjoyed. I had been so consumed by trying to fit into this ideal vision of what a mom should be that I lost sight of what really mattered. My son was happy and healthy. I needed to be happy and healthy too.

I needed to make sleep a priority for myself as well. I needed to set time aside in the day to reboot and just relax. While I hated the idea of having to ask for help, I sat down with my husband so we can come up with a better plan. Asking for help is not a sign of weakness or that you are doing anything wrong. Quite the opposite. It means you know you are struggling and want to do better; many times, we need our loved ones to step up a little more so we aren't doing it all on our own.

There will be setbacks and obstacles to overcome. We need to be flexible enough to know when something needs to be changed so that both parents and baby are happy and healthy. We want to teach our children everything they need to learn to become fully functional and happy adults. If we aren't modeling that, it is going to be more difficult to believe in our ability to teach these life lessons.

Happy Parents Control Their Feelings and Emotions

It is easy for parents to lose patience and their temper when they are not getting enough sleep themselves. Create a plan that allows both parents, or one parent and another family member, to step in to allow for the other partner to catch up on sleep. Prior to committing to a sleep coaching plan, you need to have realistic goals and the support in place to ensure that you, yourself, are getting enough sleep.

Also, keep in mind that we are working towards making progress with sleep behaviors and these don't have a definite time-frame. You will find that even if you get your little one sleeping through the night, you may need to help them through their sleep struggles for years to come. There are bound to be hiccups, regressions, and life events that can catch everyone off guard. Focus on making progress one step at a time, so that both you and baby are getting enough sleep and you can reach the ultimate end goal.

Another thing that needs to be addressed is how we communicate with our children. No matter what age they are, effective communication is essential when it comes to parenting. Since most children are unable to express their needs in a functional way until they are older, parents need to be able to express what is expected of them in a clear and compassionate manner. We need to control our emotions when dealing with emotional topics – that is what makes us adults. Children can't do this so it's up to us to learn strategies to use our emotions to help us communicate instead of complicating matters even further.

Parents also need to have a better understanding of what developmental milestone they can expect their child to meet. The problem many parents run into is that they have high expectations of their kids and often forget that they are still raising a child. Parents may impose strict rules and guidelines for their children to follow, for instance, even if they are not old enough to understand consequences. We need to remember, too, that our children will react to our negative emotions with more negativity. Instead of providing them with more chaos, we can provide them with more calm.

Accidental parenting is a type of parenting that results from constantly relying on quick fixes for issues we might have with our children. These quick fixes often turn into long-term habits that the baby and young children rely on. Many parents rely on these quick fixes when they are depleted, drained, and have no more left to give. Others turn to them because they are simply easier than battling with their child, once again, to get to sleep without the constant tears and wails.

When we fall into this trap of accidental parenting, we tend to repeat the actions that provide us with instant gratification. We know this is rarely a step up from having to buckle down and be consistent with efforts. We convince ourselves that simply nursing our little one to sleep at the beginning of bedtime is far easier than having to fight to get them to sleep on their own. Then, we suffer from having to wake up multiple times throughout the night to repeat these actions, over and over, to get them back to sleep. In the short-term and long-term, you and baby are both losing precious sleep.

Accidental parenting can occur at any age or stage. It is what happens when we regularly waiver from a structured routine. It happens when we sing one more song that turns into a whole Broadway musical. We are not providing the support and encouragement that will allow our children to learn and develop the skills that will help them in the long run. It also doesn't provide them with the security that nurtures the confidence to thrive on their own.

What is worse, accidental parenting tends to set us back weeks, if not months, even when we had been making or seeing a great deal of progress. This is due to the confusion your baby goes through when you are sticking with one thing, then suddenly "give-up" and throw an old familiar thing back into the mix.

Dennise came to me when she was struggling to get her daughter, Lori, to sleep through the night a little after her first birthday. Until then, her daughter had been a decent little sleeper. After 7 months, Lori was sleeping through the night for the most part, but now, all of a sudden, she was waking every couple of hours.

Dennise had a highly-stressful job. She was working slightly longer hours in the day because of a big project her company was wrapping up. When she would get home, she would spend as much time with Lori as possible but she was often exhausted. Then, Lori began to resist going to sleep in the evening. Out of desperation, Dennise fell back to giving her daughter a bottle before bed. She knew that doing so would get her to sleep quickly and Dennise needed sleep as well but Lori would then be up in just a few hours. Again, she would revert to the old habit of getting Lori to fall back to sleep as quickly as possible.

After a few nights of reintroducing this old habit, Dennise was losing more sleep and so was Lori. They were both miserable. Unfortunately, this meant Dennise would have to take the time to wean her daughter of the bottle before bed, once again.

Dennise did what many parents tend to do. We go to what has worked in the past, not considering how ineffective it actually is. The more we rely on these accidental parenting techniques, the more struggle we will have with our children in teaching them a skill that they will benefit from.

Avoiding these traps takes commitment. When you align your commitment with your conscious parenting style, you will find that it is much easier to sidestep the accidental parenting setbacks and continue on the path to progress.

CHAPTER 10:

HOW TO CHOOSE THE BEST SLEEP COACHING STRATEGY AND STICK WITH IT

We have been going from one sleep method to another and nothing seems to be working. Our little Debra just doesn't seem to be ready to sleep on her own. We have tried bumping up her bedtime, pushing it back, rocking to sleep, singing to sleep, fading out of the room, moving her back into our room, sleeping in her room with her...We start with one method and when it doesn't work, we put a halt on sleep training thinking she just isn't there yet. Then we wait a few weeks and try a new method. I am afraid that we have tried everything and have run out of ideas about what to do. We all need more sleep, but when will she be ready? -Ashlee.

Your sleep coaching strategy choice is very important, and it can depend on many internal and external factors. Parents should always be ready to switch to another if the previous or current strategy is not effective. However, when you are using a strategy that has shown overall positive results, it's best to stick to it, even if there is a short-term setback. How successful any sleeping coaching method is, depends almost completely on how much confidence you have in your own abilities. So, it's important that you follow through, and are persistent when encouraging proper sleep habits for your child(ren).

To Teach or not to Teach

Sleeping is not an easy skill to teach. There are so many internal and external factors that can hinder or promote healthy sleep, as we've covered in this book. It is very easy to become overwhelmed with making the best choices that will provide our babies with a safe and ideal sleep environment.

A sleep coaching plan focuses first on your baby's needs. You may be looking for ways, for instance, to eliminate nighttime feeding. Maybe you've tried to wean your baby off of the extra feeding but they keep waking up every few hours. As you have learned, this can be caused by any number of factors that have nothing to do with hunger. Sleep coaching begins by tracking your baby's natural sleeping and feeding habits which lets you see the big picture more clearly. You are able to better identify what might be the root cause of your baby's sleep struggles and formulate a long-term plan that addresses these issues.

Tracking your baby's natural cycles is one factor of a sleep coaching plan. The other factor accounts for your baby's personality and their specific characteristics and temperament. This helps you see what external factors may be causing your baby distress and be contributing to poor sleeping habits. You also learn to connect with your baby on a deeper level by seeing their true personality.

Finally, sleep coaching lets you customize a plan that fits with your family's needs. As parents, of course, we want our baby to sleep better.

When I had my third son, my husband and I had to completely change our approach to sleep coaching. With two other boys under the age of five, a new baby was going to disrupt all of our sleep if we didn't address what we needed from day one. We devised a plan that would allow us to include our other two boys in the baby's bedtime routine.

They would read to him or take care of dimming the lights and closing the curtains. It was important for us to involve our older boys in the routine so they didn't feel neglected. We also adjusted their routines so that when we put the new baby to sleep, they had plenty of quiet activities to keep them busy before starting on their own bedtime routines. We all took turns tucking our new family members into bed, sharing responsibility, and giving everyone the time they needed to stay calm and relaxed. We never felt overwhelmed and everyone got the sleep they needed.

Make a Preliminary Sleep Coaching Plan

Creating a sleep coaching plan is not something easily done in one sitting. Take the time to figure out how the sleep coaching plan will work for the baby, and the family:

- How does your baby's sleep impact the family?
- What is the one thing you want to change about your baby's sleep habits?
- What is a realistic sleeping goal for your baby, appropriate for their age?
- If your baby was to sleep better, how would that have a positive impact on your daily lives?
- How would getting your baby on a consistent napping and sleep schedule affect your family?

- How does the view you have on your parenting abilities affect your own well-being and confidence?

The answers to these questions can help you come to a more realistic view of what troubles your baby may be having, and how that might be affecting the family unit.

Setting goals that are ideal, realistic, and cater to your unique family's needs will result in a more effective sleep coaching program. Determining what goals you should be focusing on can be done by taking the below steps:

1. Begin by tracking your baby's current sleep patterns. When do they wake up in the morning, feed, nap, poop, and fall asleep in the evening? How many times do they wake up in the middle of the night?
2. Start a bedtime routine that takes into account the information you've gleaned from the first step.

3. Track how you usually get your baby to sleep. What activities do they need, who is in the room, where do they sleep?
4. Is the sleep environment one that encourages sleep?
5. Talk to your pediatrician if you have any concerns about your baby's sleep.

Once you have tracked your baby's sleep patterns for two weeks and stuck with a bedtime routine, you have probably identified a few things that can be changed immediately. Now, it is time to choose your start-date. Ensure that, as you are going through the sleep coaching process, there will be no interruptions like vacations or family visits. When it's time to begin, keep a detailed log on how it's going, so you can track the progress you are making.

How to Switch from One Strategy to Another

If your baby is happy, healthy, and their sleep patterns are not causing stress or lack of sleep for others in the home, then the routine appears to be an ideal fit. If, on the other hand, your baby's sleep patterns are becoming problematic, then there is probably a need to make a change. Keep in mind, switching should not occur if there have been major life changes such as a recent move, vacation, or there has been a change in the parent's work schedule that causes them to be in the home less often. Only if you have been consistent with your efforts with an alternative sleep training method, and have not seen progress, will you consider switching.

Reevaluate where your baby is in their development. Maybe stopping for a few weeks and then retrying will be a more appropriate time. Trying to force your child to adhere to a strict sleeping routine when they are not ready will only set you and your baby up for problems. If you haven't seen any progress or positive changes in your baby's sleep after four weeks, then it might be best to switch up to a new plan.

You may find that you need to take a firmer approach to your sleep coaching method if your baby is resisting a great deal. Switching methods can be confusing to your baby which is why it is not recommended, unless absolutely necessary. Before deciding to give up on your current method, keep in mind your baby's temperament, any underlying issues that can have an impact on your success and your own emotional health.

When switching:

- Check-in with your pediatrician
- Review your child's concerning behaviors
- See if anything needs to be changed in their environment
- Consider how your parenting strategies might need to change

- Have any unexpected life changes been hindering your efforts?

I had been working with the Miller family for about a month. They were transitioning their baby, Ashton, into his own room but doing so resulted in weeks of sleepless nights. Ashton would fall asleep easily at the beginning of the night but would wake up every hour, unable to go back to sleep without mom or dad in the room. Mom and Dad had been using a gradual method, removing themselves from the room so Ashton would fall asleep by himself. They weren't making progress and there was no other reason that could explain his constant wakings throughout the night. I suggested they move Ashton back into their room for a week and, instead of jumping right into placing Ashton into his own room, they gradually moved his bed closer to his own room.

Every few days they would move his crib further away from their bed; then, just outside their bedroom. When they reached his room, mom and dad would alternate sleeping by his bed for the first week. Then they were able to go every other day without having to sleep in his room. Eventually, Ashton was able to soothe himself back to sleep with no one in the room when he woke in the middle of the night.

Sometimes, just the smallest change in your plan can make all the difference. These changes may result in having to take more steps to get your baby to sleep on their own but will get you there faster than sticking with a plan that doesn't work.

CONCLUSION

Baby Bootcamp: Sleep Training for a Happy Healthy Baby, provides you with the best techniques, tips, and solutions for the most common sleep issues you are bound to encounter as a new parent. From the time you bring the baby home, and even when they are out in the world on their own, they will turn to you for comfort and security. Bedtimes are the ideal time to provide these basic emotional needs for your child.

This book has covered a variety of topics that will strengthen the bond between you and your baby, while also ensuring they remain healthy by getting the quality sleep they need. You have learned, in the first chapter, the key differences between infant sleep and adult sleep, as well as how these change as they grow. In the second chapter, you discovered some of the best sleep training methods you can implement from day one to teach your baby how to sleep independently. You also learned which methods work best, according to your infant's age and development.

Chapter 3 taught you the importance of the right sleep schedule and bedtime routines. These are key components that your child will utilize for the rest of their lives. In Chapter 4, we covered how to create the safest sleep environment for you baby. You learned how to reduce the risk of SIDS by taking into consideration all the factors that make up your baby's sleep environment.

Chapters 5 through 8 covered all the things that can hinder a child's sleep. The information provided in these chapters, I hope, has helped you better understand the internal and external factors that can cause sleep disturbances, when to expect these issues to arise, and how to combat them.

The final two chapters dove into how to stay mentally strong while dealing with regression, health issues, and troublesome behavior. These chapters provide you with encouragement, support, and the truth behind how your parenting techniques can eliminate or increase prolonged sleep problems, for you and your child.

Sleep coaching isn't just about your baby getting the sleep they need. These methods take into consideration what the parents and family need.

You are not alone in your baby sleep battle. All parents suffer through sleepless nights and end up hoping that, one day, restful sleep will return. You don't have to wait until your child is older. Bedtime doesn't have to be a burden and it doesn't have to be a nightmare. While teaching your baby to sleep on their own takes commitment and patience, it can mean that bedtime is a joyous time that you all look forward to.

When we combine old-school and new methods, as covered in this book, we can help your baby build healthy, lifelong sleep habits.

Remember:

- Start by tracking your baby's natural sleep cycle and their sleep cues
- Create a calming bedtime routine that you can use for years to come
- Set up the right sleep environment
- Be consistent

These four simple steps can move you from a place of stress and anxiety around bedtime to a place of compassion and understanding.

I hope that what I've learned as a parent will help you. In the very least, you know that you're not alone. You can now begin sleep coaching with confidence. Remember to remain patient and stay in tune with your own emotions as well as your baby's. This will lead you to success when it comes to your baby sleeping comfortably through the night.

Now all you have to do is get started! I wish you the best of luck on your parental journey; know that I am here to help.

REFERENCES

Brain Basics: Understanding Sleep. (n.d.). Retrieved from https://www.ninds.nih.gov/disorders/Patient-Caregiver-Education/

Carberg, J. (2019, May 3). Postpartum depression statistics. Retrieved from https://www.postpartumdepression.org/resources/statistics/

Chamberlin, J. (2004, February.). *Sleep, baby, sleep.* Retrieved from https://www.apa.org/monitor/feb04/sleep

Dubief, A. (2017). Precious little sleep: the complete baby sleep guide for modern parents. Essex Junction, VT: Lomhara Press.

Flynn-Evans, E. (2020, April 15). Early vs. Late Bedtime-Which is right? Strategies to shift bedtime to. Retrieved from https://www.babysleepscience.com/single-post/2014/04/08/Early-vs-Late-Bedtime-Which-is-Right-How-to-use-Early-and-Late-bedtimes-to-solve-common-sleep-problems

Franck, L., Gay, C. L., Lynch, M., and Lee, K. A. (2011, December). Infant sleep after immunization: randomized controlled trial of prophylactic acetaminophen. Retrieved from https://www.ncbi.nlm.nih.gov/pmc/articles/PMC3387894/

Hookway, L. (2018). Holistic Sleep Coaching - Gentle Alternatives to Sleep Training: for health & childcare professionals. Place of publication not identified: PRAECLARUS Press.

Karp, H. D. (2002). The happiest baby. England: Michael Joseph.

Mezrah, S. (2010). The baby sleeps tonight. Naperville, IL: Sourcebooks.

Pediatric Sleep Disorders. (n.d.). Retrieved from https://stanfordhealthcare.org/medical-conditions/sleep/pediatric-sleep-disorders.html

Research on Possible Causes Of SIDS. (n.d.).

Retrieved from https://safetosleep.nichd.nih.gov/research/science/causes#triple

Sears, W., Sears, R., & Sears, M. (2005). The baby sleep book: how to help your baby sleep and have a restful night. London: Thorsons.

Signs and Symptoms of Autism Spectrum Disorders. (2019, August 27). Retrieved from https://www.cdc.gov/ncbddd/autism/signs.html

Sleeping like a baby: Sleep in the first years of life. (n.d.). Retrieved from https://thepsychologist.bps.org.uk/sleeping-baby-sleep-first-years-life

Tarullo, A. R., Balsam, P. D., & Fifer, W. P. (2011, January 1). Sleep and Infant Learning. Retrieved from https://www.ncbi.nlm.nih.gov/pmc/articles/PMC3034475/

Understanding-Sleepdefault - Stanford Children's Health. (n.d.). Retrieved from https://www.stanfordchildrens.org/en/topic/default?id=gastrointestinal-problems-90-P02216